Jump Up

Jump Up

Good Times Throughout the seasons with Celebrations from Around the World

Luisah Teish

Foreword by *Angeles Arrien, Ph. D.*

CONARI
PRESS

Conari Press books are distributed by Publishers Group West.

Excerpts from GUMBO YA-YA by Lyle Saxon. Copyright 1945, © renewed 1973 by the Louisiana State Library. Reprinted by permission of Houghton Mifflin Company. All rights reserved.

Excerpt from Wheel of the Year by Pauline Campanelli. Copyright © 1989 by Pauline Campanelli. Reprinted by pernission of Pauline Campanelli.

Some of the material in this book is reprinted from *Carnival of the Spirit,* by Luisah Teish.

ISBN: 1-57324-551-8

Cover Illustrations: Kathleen Edwards
Author Photo: Gay Block
Cover Design: Ame Beanland
Interior Illustrations: Luisah Teish
Interior chapter opening shells: Kathleen Edwards
Book Design: Suzanne Albertson

Library of Congress Cataloging-in-Publication Data

Teish, Luisah.
Jump up : seasonal celebrations from the world's deep traditions /Luisah Teish.
p.   cm.
Includes bibliographical references and index.
ISBN 1–57324–551–8
1. Festivals. 2. Festival—Africa. I. Title.
GT3930 .T43 2000
394.26—dc21   00–010168

Printed in the United States of America on recycled paper.

00 01 02   BIS   10 9 8 7 6 5 4 3 2 1

To Damballah Hwedo, the Rainbow Serpent

To the Ancestors: My elder the Iyalode of Oshogbo, Nigeria

My sister, Ms. Joyce M. E. L. Robinson

To my longtime friend, Rev. Norma Tringali

And to kindred spirits everywhere!

JUMP UP

ƒOREWORD

by *Angeles Arrien, Ph.D.*, cultural anthropologist,
author of *The Four-Fold Way* and *Signs of Life*

To many people, the ideals of the Industrial Revolution—the never-ending desire for more progress, more development, and greater wealth—no longer seem relevant to our modern lives, yet we have trouble letting them go. If we are to survive in the world of the twenty-first century, however, we must reconsider our priorities.

The great historian Arnold Toynbee, through his analysis of the rise and fall of twenty civilizations, offers a larger perspective on the current shifts in values and lifestyles. Summarizing the principles of civilization's growth, Toynbee formulated the Law of Progressive Simplification, which reminds us that the measure of a civilization's growth and sustainable vitality lies in its ability to transfer increasing amounts of energy and attention away from the material side of life toward the educational, psychological, cultural, aesthetic, and spiritual sides.

Luisah Teish's lifelong commitment has been to foster growth and sustainable vitality within the human spirit. *Jump Up* is not only an invitation to practice and celebrate Toynbee's Law of Progressive Simplification, it offers us as well a wealth of worldwide seasonal holidays, rituals, ceremonies, stories, and ancient practices that amplify and honor the transformational opportunities available to us each season.

Educator Parker Palmer reminds us what a powerful symbol each season is for the movement of life: It suggests that life is neither a battlefield nor a game of chance, but something infinitely richer, more promising, more real. The notion that our lives are like the eternal cycle of the seasons does not deny the struggle or the joy, the loss or the gain, the darkness or the light, but encourages us to embrace it all—and to find in all of it opportunities for growth.

Throughout recorded history all cultures have devised rituals as a means of handling life's changes. Every society uses ritual to acknowledge the major life transitions of birth, initiation, marriage, and death. The word *ritual,* in fact, derives from an Indo-European root meaning "to fit together." It is related to such words as *art, skill, order, weaving,* and *arithmetic,* all of which involve fitting things together to create order. Luisah Teish provides us with a seasonal handbook that helps us create a way through sacred intention and conscious actions to fit things together. Essentially, *Jump Up* is a book that supports making people healthier and happier, and Luisah's great gift is to remind us that life is a mystery to be celebrated and that magic is always afoot.

PREfACE

Jump up is a term used as an expression of great joy. Most often it refers to an event that includes joyous music, laughter, food, and dancing. So we may have a Jump Up to celebrate a special occasion. It also refers to the act of dancing with abandon, as we do at Mardi Gras in New Orleans and the Carnivals of Brazil, Jamaica, and San Francisco. *Jump up* is a relative of several other joyous expressions. In celebration we find ourselves jumping, jamming, swinging, hopping, and kicking it.

Whether it is an event or an action, *jump up* always implies an outward expression of inner joy. This joy comes not merely from a set of circumstances, such as the decorations or the food, but is an outpouring of a feeling that resides deep within a person, a community, or a culture.

All the spiritual cultures of the world have holidays that are designed to celebrate our relationship to Spirit, to Nature, and to each other. On these occasions we recognize that we are children of the Earth responding to changes in the Earth by participating in celebrations of the seasons. We also acknowledge the life and work of illustrious ancestors who have given us the culture we've inherited and the celebrations we observe. This book helps us to celebrate the seasons and these ancestors. It is written for people who want to feel themselves a part of the larger family and community of the world.

This year, as in every year, many of us will find satisfaction in repeating ceremonial acts that have been prescribed by our culture and religion for centuries. Some of us will honor the ways of the past but may also find that the familiar celebrations have lost their meaning, or that the meaning has become obscured by gross commercialism. We may find that we have a need for something that goes deeper, that is more personal and more directly related to our desires and experiences.

This book is written for the person who wants to understand the meaning of traditional holidays such as Christmas and Easter. By examining the mythology and the symbolism of these holidays, you will come to understand the meaning of Yule logs and rabbits who peddle chicken eggs. We will go into the depth of the past, and the celebrations will become more meaningful to you. We will come to know what our ancestors knew and how these celebrations came to be.

The traditional holidays are based on earlier celebrations of the Equinoxes and the Solstices, which charted the movement of the Sun and its relationship to life on Planet Earth. Winter officially begins with the Solstice on December 21. It is the longest night of the year. Thereafter, night diminishes and day increases until they are equally balanced at the Spring Equinox. On March 21, day begins to increase and continues its ascendancy until June 21—the Summer Solstice, the longest day of the year. Then the Sun yields its power until night and day are equal again, at the Autumn Equinox on September 21. This cycle is the Joyous Dance of Winter, Spring, Summer, Autumn, Winter, and Spring again. This is the Natural Cycle of gestation, growth, fullness, and harvest. How these are celebrated in Western culture will be explored.

Perhaps a greater gift of this book is to introduce the reader to a wide variety of celebrations from many cultures in the world. We will participate in the African American celebration of Kwanzaa, the Mexican celebration of Diá de Los Muertos (Day of the Dead), and the Chinese celebration of Mooncakes and Hungry Ghosts. You will meet the deities of Africa, Europe, Asia, and the Americas who helped shape the natural world. The trees that inhabit the rainforest and the animals that roam the plains will play with you, and the ancestors of ancient times will tell you their stories. Then you will be encouraged to explore the beautiful landscape of your own dreams and desires, and from that deep place to create celebrations that are truly meaningful and joyous.

A Calendar is provided at the end of the book, so that you may tune in to the celebrations that are happening somewhere in the world every day. And, if you wish, you can participate with them in your own home.

In each chapter I share the stories of my personal travels. I invite you to come with me on a camel ride across the Giza plateau in Egypt, to climb up the rocks and then down into a cave in Jamaica, and to jump up with me in an African village. In this way I can share the continuing adventures of my quest for joy and kinship. By sharing these experiences we can jump up around the globe. You will mingle with the people, feel their joy, and share in their mystery.

At the end of each chapter you will find examples of celebrations I have conducted in diverse communities with great success. Here you will find guidelines for creating your own celebrations.

And because food, like music, is such an important part of the celebration, I have made at least one serving suggestion for each season and have included recipes. Some will be familiar to you; others come from cookpots in foreign corners of the world. I have also listed a few cookbooks where other recipes can be found.

So pull out the cloth and the candles, bake the bread and arrange the flowers, gather together, then go deeply into the beauty of Nature and contemplate the mystery of Spirit, and when you emerge from the deep, put on the music and jump up.

INTRODUCTION

My Own Path Toward Celebration

As a child I enjoyed the fuss and fanfare of the holidays. Thanksgiving and Christmas were always big affairs in my mother's household, especially in the kitchen. We never made a lot of fuss over the Christmas tree or the Easter baskets. The dinner table and the food were the main attractions. We took a fold-up table out of the closet and pushed it flush with the kitchen table. The table was set with a linen cloth, blue-patterned plates, silverware, the "good" glasses, and a bottle of Manischewitz or Mogen David wine. My mother never allowed any other wine on the table. She said it was "holy" wine. As a child I knew nothing about kosher products and still do not know how we came to respect a Jewish tradition in a Black Catholic household.

On holidays our kitchen and living room became "the front room," where eating, dancing, singing, and general socializing took place. The "back room" (the bedrooms) became the nursery and dorm in which children and elders could lie down, and the bathroom remained itself. The house was magically transformed with pieces of cloth and lampshades, and with bowls of fruit and nuts laid about.

But the real magic was the cooking. It took several days to prepare all the food. The turkey would slowly be thawed out, and the neck, liver, and gizzard removed. The neck would then be thrown in a pot to boil until the meat fell off the bone. This meat was minced and put aside in a bowl. Later it would be stirred into brown gravy made of turkey stock and flour.

A big pan of cornbread was made, unleavened but with lots of butter. It would be set aside while my sisters and I chopped seasoning for the dressing: yellow and green onions, celery, garlic, and bell peppers. Moma would sprinkle black pepper and seasoning salt with minced garlic on the inside and outside of the turkey. Then we'd put the unbaked turkey in the refrigerator for a few hours to "let the seasoning settle in." We referred to him as "Mr. Turkey" and told him how good he would look and taste when cooked. The unleavened cornbread and chopped seasoning would be mixed together with oysters, shrimp, or sausage, moistened with turkey stock, and sprinkled with sage. Voilà! This was homemade dressing. The dressing would be stuffed in the belly and neck cavity of the turkey, and then the bird would be drizzled with seasoned butter and covered with a wet tea towel. The pot was covered and placed in a slow oven so that the turkey cooked overnight. Several times this pot would be opened to the sound of *oohs* and *aahs* and the smell of wonder.

This journey into the world of holiday cooking began on Thanksgiving with the turkey and ended on New Year's with

Creole cabbage. Holiday cooking usually took about three days for each holiday. What a ritual it was! There was the business of how fine or how coarse to chop this or that vegetable. We watched yeast dough rise and get punched down again. At some point Aunt Marybelle Reed, ("Ibae," a salutation of blessing for those who have passed over) or Miz Theresa would come by to debate the virtues of butter versus oleo or try their best to get my mother to eat something that she considered taboo. It never worked. A large pot of hot eggnog was made; neighbors dropped by to have a glass (with brandy or rum), report their cooking progress, fuss about something in the news, or recount stories that had changed some small but significant thing about their lives.

I remember the food and the socializing as the great things about the holidays—seeing Aunt So-and-So and tasting her all-butter pound cake, smelling the cigar smoke in the next room where the uncles exaggerated their exploits and the aunts laughed about how fast the children were growing and what a cute thing Johnny, Jr., did the other day, holding the new baby and feeling the soft warmth of her touch, being inside where it was warm with food and friends.

We children knew that the packages under the Christmas tree would be clothes. In low-income families clothes were the good gift. In fact, I remember a year when a local Catholic group gave toys away. Each child walked down a long assembly line of things and was allowed to choose an item. I selected a hula hoop, and my friends made it clear that they thought this toy was a silly choice.

The holidays were also a time to extend ourselves to those who were less fortunate, because we did, after all, have food, shelter, and each other. So we looked in on the old folks, forgave the people who'd offended us, and resolved that something was going to be different somehow. Somewhere in this agenda church fit in: a midnight mass, a sunrise service, listening to the choir wail, and watching the appropriate Bible movie on television.

When I grew older and left home, I was thrown into circles of people who treated the holidays differently. There was less emphasis on food and clothes, more emphasis on money and things. Being at home together was not as important as being in the "right" place, being seen with the "cool people." As adolescence stretched out into young adulthood, I watched the holidays become a time of false piety, social snobbery, and conspicuous consumption. By the time I reached college I'd taken a political position against the holidays—period. They were just another excuse to beat people out of their money, lay somebody off a job, tell another lie about the past, bow down to a White baby boy, look up to a bleeding statue, or act out strange behaviors without understanding what they meant. This was followed by my "Black pride and awareness" period. To give meaning to an otherwise meaningless year, I turned everything Black. Jesus, Mary, and Joseph became Black, even Easter became Black. That winter holiday was now spelled *Xmas* to indicate the unknown truth. New Year's remained nebulous, while Thanksgiving became the "Criminals' Holiday," on which I railed against exploitation of Native Americans.

In the late '60s my quest for spiritual liberation began with Egypt, the wonderful, mystical cradle of civilization. I joined the Fahamme Temple of Amun-Ra in St. Louis, where I learned Egyptian beliefs about the Solstices and Equinoxes, was taught to analyze the symbols associated with holidays, and was made to understand that the daily rising and setting of the Sun make each day a "holy day." I felt a little better.

The quest for cosmic joy took me to Africa, where the deities walk among human beings and dance *is* worship. In studying Africa I learned that the strength of a culture will endure even the greatest hardships and still retain its beauty and power. Centuries ago the transatlantic slave trade, which was sponsored by the Catholic Church, brought millions of Black people from their Motherland, Africa, to the so-called New World. We were dispersed throughout the Western Hemisphere, with large concentrations in Brazil, the Caribbean Islands, and the North American colonies. Slavery required that these Africans be baptized, take Christian names, and worship the saints. At the same time the Black Codes, which regulated plantation behavior, forbade slaves to marry, to own property, to speak their own languages, or to worship and celebrate in their own fashion. However, the attempt to destroy African culture did not succeed. Like most people, we managed to acclimate ourselves to the land, people, and culture around us, and in the process we created rituals and celebrations that are both old and new. This is the creative gift of African American culture.

Later I was blessed with the opportunity to experience some of the ceremonies of Native American spiritual culture, which call us to walk in balance upon the Earth, to regard Her as our Mother, and to take care of Her. This point of view resonates with the African belief that we are children of Nature who can and must turn to the Water, the Thunder, and the Mountains for strength, guidance, and joy. I came to realize that the African and Native American traditions are blessed with elders who could teach me the stories and rituals that have been preserved in spite of centuries of oppression.

As I became more involved in the Women's Spirituality Movement, my friend and sister Starhawk introduced me to the pagan tradition. At last what seemed to have been mere nonsense began to make real common sense. I came to understand that paganism is the ancestral tradition of European culture, from which the traditions of Christianity were born.

I now live in a racially diverse neighborhood in Oakland, California—a community in which I am dedicated to living joyfully. With the help of imagination I have created a wonderland in my own home and life. My work as a performer, writer, and ritual designer also takes me to sacred sites all over the world. The blessing of my experience is that I have found kindred spirits to jump up with everywhere. I have learned that every day is a Holy Day. And the Earth is a sacred place where the power of the Sea and the beauty of the Sky express Mother Nature's love for humanity and the wonder of Creation. I feel so very blessed, and in sharing this blessing with you, I invite you to create a beautiful world every day of your year, every day of your life.

I have stood silently in awe of the rainforest
in Africa, the South Pacific, and the Caribbean.
I've walked down dusty roads in Mexico and
said prayers to the Pyramid of the Moon.
I've watched the volcano erupt and
followed Her lava flow to the sea in Hawaii.
I've swung from ancient vines in the caves of Jamaica and buried
the dead in Dakar.
I've danced with delight around totem poles and pressed my fore-
head to that of Maori warriors.
I have eaten strange fruit and wild flowers in Australia and bathed in
the waters of the Rhine.
I've joked with the pale fox in the crossroads, then wrestled with the
Jaguar and won.
I have embraced great trees between my thighs, spoke words of love
to thunder while riding lightning bolts.
I have danced on the pyramids in Egypt, howled at the moon on
the Avila Mountains of Venezuela.
I have dreamed with the souls in Atlantis.

—Luisah Teish

7

Myths
and Deities

In the beginning, at a time when there was no Time, all that existed was the great silence in the dark depth of the Cosmic Womb (Nana Buluku). Within the Womb, the Great Egg of the World (Olodumare) sat in patient potential waiting for the fated moment of Its hatching. Suddenly a sound burst out from the center of the egg—OOORRRROOO—and the life-giving particles in the egg quickened and set into motion a tremendous bang, causing creative air spirits in the form of gases to dance among themselves. They danced themselves into Fire; they danced themselves into Earth. In the frenzy of their joy, Moon (Mawu) and Sun (Lisa) were born. Other dancing gases clashed and collided into fireballs spinning through the deep blue of space. They leaped and tumbled into the luminous depth of the Earth and formed the Ocean (Yemaya-Olokun). The rushing hum of the Ocean splashed Itself against Earth's shores, as the great masses of land erupted from Her depth (Odudua).

Sun stepped forward to perform His solo, and the Moon laid back to cool Herself off in the Upper Deep. As the Sun performed His slow drag over the surface of the Earth, life stirred in His rays (Ache). In the depth of the Sea, things began to form—a single

Myths
and Deities

The Serpent wrapped itself around the Earth and the Sky, holding the two together like a covered calabash.

cell divided into two making seaweed, hydra, and fish. The crab crawled out of the water and found that on the land, life was moving. Seed burst open, forming flowers, trees, and fruit. Spiders crawled, birds flew, and bush cows roamed in the forest. A blazing heat permeated the Earth, causing all things to stir and take shape. But the Sun's heat was overwhelming; things were being overdone, so He receded, and the Moon brought forth Her dance. She circled slowly through the night sky cooling the Earth, settling seed, calming the waters, and leaking a mysterious ray of subtle light (Ache) that tempered everything on Earth.

The Moon called out, alarmed by the magnitude of the work they had done. Her cry resounded to the depths of the Earth, and up from the center came the Rainbow Serpent (Damballah Hwedo). The Serpent wrapped Itself around the Earth and the Sky, holding the two together like a covered calabash. Sun and Moon smiled at the work of the Serpent. Within Its Ring of Power the Celestial Couple made love and brought into being all the deities as twins. And on the planet's surface the palm and banana trees swayed in the wind, birds sang, fish swam, and the bush cows roamed in the garden.

This myth is a blending of two West African myths. It is a composite of the Creation stories of the Fon People of Dahomey (Republic of Benin) and the Yoruba people of southwest Nigeria. Throughout this book, I have used the names of deities from these cultures to personify Cosmic forces and have merged this myth into some corresponding modern beliefs about the Universe. This story contains the same elements as can be found in the mythologies of most of the world's people. The greatest similarity among the world's creation myths lies in the attempt to explain how things were "in the beginning." Some stories, like those of the Maori people of New Zealand (Aotaeroa), put great emphasis on the Nothingness that existed before Creation. In the beginning there is a Void, and in the Void there is a small but powerful potential. It may be a spark of Light, a seed, or an egg. That small potential is so full of power that it causes a turbulence of some kind. There is a sound, perhaps "the Word" is spoken by a Great Deity, and then the Light Show begins. In this version of the myth, our beginnings are cracked from the Cosmic Egg. It erupts and explodes from darkness to light. The Sun, Moon, and Stars spring from the bowels or the heads of deities. They crawl out of holes in the ether. Water splashes, land erupts, things grow, fly, swim, and roam. And after a time, Human Beings show up for the party.

It erupts and explodes from darkness to light.

All the myths speak of the relationships between Creator and Creation, between Humans and the Natural World. And every culture designs its calendar, its art, its rituals, and its celebrations according to the beliefs set forth in its mythology.

The World's Myths

Most of the world's holidays are based on ancient myths. I am using the word *myth* to describe stories that attempt to explain Universal Truth in symbolic language. Unfortunately, the popular notion of myth mistakenly defines it as a simple untruth. Actually, myths are the cornerstone of Spirituality and Religion, their rituals and traditions. Real myth impacts culture at every level. It shapes political perspective and social structure. It determines our attitudes and actions toward the Earth, the natural world, and each other. Even science and its explorations are influenced by the cultural symbols and ideals found in myth.

Myths of Origin tell us why and how a particular tradition

came into being. Usually these stories are populated with supernatural beings such as deities or mythological beasts, and they feature the actions of heroic human ancestors. So we find a genesis myth that tells us to tend a garden (the Earth) and to offer the fruits of our labor (to sacrifice) to a deity who is responsible for its existence. This is the origin of Harvest Festivals. We also have stories about exceptional human beings, infused with spiritual power, who with the guidance and support of deities are empowered to perform extraordinary feats, such as virgin birth and triumph over death. We celebrate these stories and characters because they have a significant impact on how we live life on Earth.

In all myths everywhere, the Earth is called "Our Mother," "Mother Nature," and "The Great Mother Goddess." Her name is Gaia in the traditions of Europe, Haumea—or Papa to Native Hawaiians—and Asase Yaa among the people of Ghana. Many aspects of Nature—the wind, water, forest, and fire—are given male and female attributes in human culture. But most often, the Earth is seen as a Woman in various stages of life, with self-renewing powers.

In Spring, the Earth is seen as a young Maiden wearing wildflowers in her hair. This is the Greek Persephone and the African Goddess Oshun, Daughter of Promise. In Summer, when the Sun is brightest, Isis of Egypt and other Mothers of Light bring forth the fullness of the flowers, Their beautiful children who adorn the Earth for celebration. She is seen as Mother-Woman. In Autumn, when the crops are ripe for picking, She becomes Ceres, Queen of the Harvest, the Abundant Provider. But when the multicolored leaves fall and seeds fly through the air, She becomes Oya, the Amazon Goddess of the Winds of Change. In Northern climates, Grandmother Earth may sleep or appear to die in Winter, but in tropical climates She is the Pregnant Mother gestating in the quiet depths awaiting the moment of rebirth in Spring.

As we move through the seasons in this book, you will meet many mythological and historical figures who personify the powers of Nature and exemplify human intelligence and courage. Some of the stories and figures associated with major Western holidays are probably familiar to you, whereas others may be completely new. Following is a brief introduction to the cast of characters and a sampling of some of the myths that surround them.

The Deities

Nana Buluku: Nana Buluku is the Primal Darkness, the Great Mother of the Sky pantheon for the West African people of Dahomey. She is seen as gynandrous, that is, primarily female but with male potential contained within Herself. Thus, She is able to give birth to Mawu and Lisa.

Olodumare: Olodumare is the Owner of the Rainbow in Yoruba mythology (West Africa). He gives us each day, which contains a spectrum of possibilities that is as high, wide, and colorful as the rainbow we see in the sky. Olodumare is related to Olorun, the Owner of the sky.

Mawu and Lisa: Mawu and Lisa are the divine twins born from Nana Buluku. Mawu, the Moon, is feminine, old, cool, and kind. She lives in the West and has rulership over the nighttime, when humans rest. Lisa, Her twin brother, is young, hot, and fierce. He lives in the East and has rulership over the daytime with all its human activity and concerns. In the Yoruba pantheon (West Africa), the dual nature of life is personified as a set of twin children, Taiwo and Kehinde, the *Ibeji*. In Haiti they are called the *Marassa*. Ibeji-Marassa can be viewed as female/male, Moon/Sun, night/day, cool/hot, left/right, and collective/individual.

Odudua, the Earth: In Yorubaland (West Africa), Odudua is the Goddess of the Good Black Earth and the twin sister of Olorun, the Owner of the Sky. We also find a culture hero by the name of Odudua, who is the progenitor of the Yoruba people. The Igbo people call the Earth *Ala*. She is the Queen of the Yam Festival, the LawMaker, and the Judge. She gives Life, fulfillment, and Death. She is also the ruler of the Underworld.

Yemaya-Olokun: Yemaya and Olokun are the Owners of the Deep Blue Sea. In West Africa Yemonja is the owner of the Ogun River. In Brazil She is *Imanje,* the Mermaid. In the Caribbean Islands She is *Yemaya,* the Mother of the Children of the Sea, the fish. Her waves dance constantly to the rhythm of the Moon, shifting the sands, polishing the shells, and birthing the many generations of fish that feed us. *Olokun,* a deity from Benin in West Africa, is the deep and darkly mysterious part of

Myths
and Deities

the Ocean, the unfathomable realm where evolution began with the single cell. Olokun is regarded as androgynous, that is, primarily male with a female aspect contained within Himself. Together they are the salt waters of the Earth, the Secret Keepers, the Dream Weavers. Deities such as *Elusu,* the chalk-white mermaid of Togo; Papa *Densu,* also of Togo; *Agwe Taroya* of Haiti; and *Mami Wata,* who is found in West Africa and Jamaica, all share this realm with a world of mer-folks.

Damballah and Aida Hwedo: Damballah and His wife, Aida Hwedo, originate in Dahomey, West Africa, and are very popular in South America and the Caribbean Islands, especially Haiti. They are the Great Serpents, the rainbow pythons who wrap themselves around the Earth and the Sky and thereby hold the world together. The serpent is known in many cultures (including India and Australia) not as the wicked beast of Genesis, but as the wise and powerful creature that renews Itself by shedding Its skin. It is a symbol of regenerative power, sexuality, and immortality.

Obatala and Iya Mapo: These deities are not mentioned directly in the Creation myth told earlier, but they are implied. Obatala is one of the oldest deities in the Yoruba pantheon. His name means the "King of the white cloth" and refers to the clouds in the Sky, the Sunlight that shines upon the Earth, and the white light of mystic vision. In the mythology, Obatala is credited with separating the land from the waters and establishing the continents using a snail shell full of sand and a five-toed guinea hen.

He and Iya Mapo are the potter and the wet clay that shape the fetus in the Womb. One myth says that Obatala celebrated a little too much during the creation of humans, got drunk, and made a few mistakes. Because of this, Obatala holds in special favor those humans who are born with bone malformations, learning disabilities, and other congenital conditions.

Eshu-Elegba: In popular culture Eshu-Elegba is referred to as a "trickster." But the word *trickster,* which often evokes the image of a clown, is insufficient to describe His powers. He is the messenger of destiny, a deity of great importance. He serves the three major functions of Magician, Linguist, and Enforcer. As the Magician, He spins the Wheel of Fortune so that Earth, Air, Fire, Water, Time, and Space come together in varying combinations to create material reality. He is the one who allows bright ideas and devious plans to pop in and out of our minds. He also causes people and things to move together or apart. Eshu is a lascivious dancer. Eshu-Elegba is the Linguist, the Master of Communications. He interprets the thoughts, feelings, and intentions of one entity into a message that can be discerned by another. When humans sing songs or recite poetry, Elegba allows them to understand each other. Because of Him the power of music crosses cultures and "soothes the savage breast" (though sometimes it arouses the beast). In Yoruba tradition all ceremonies begin and end with an invocation to Elegba to ensure that the messages are properly delivered.

Eshu-Elegba the Enforcer is the Master of the Crossroads.

Life on Earth is a combination of destiny and choice. Within the design of Nature (the change of the seasons, the progression of life) all beings have a window of opportunity to make choices about whether or not we will grow healthily and happily, what we will birth and contribute to the world, and how we will live and die. Eshu stands in the crossroads between invisible, unperceived potentiality, and visible, material reality; between that which is going out of existence and that which is coming into being.

Persephone the Kore (young corn): Persephone is the Virgin Daughter of Demeter, the Greek Goddess of the Earth. The Greek myth states that one day, while picking flowers in the field, Persephone was abducted by the Lord of Death, who took Her beneath the Earth to Hades. On the planet's surface Demeter searched for Her daughter and, failing to find Persephone, fell into mourning. When She withdrew Her energy, the plants died, causing the other deities to demand Persephone's return. But the Lord of Death had tricked Persephone into eating three seeds from a pomegranate, and She became obligated to spend time underground with Him every year, the time that became Winter. When Persephone returns to the surface of the Earth, it is Spring and everything blossoms again.

Iyalode Oshun: Oshun is the African Venus, the Goddess of Love, Art, and Sensuality. The story states that when the world was first created Oshun ruled over all the sweet things in life.

One day, when She was bathing in the river, She overheard a group of deities gossiping about Her. Some bragged that they were stronger than She, others claimed to be smarter, while some had the nerve to imply that Her beauty was unnecessary. As a demonstration of power, Oshun left the planet and took a vacation on a nearby star, where She adorned Herself with great pleasure. Meanwhile on Earth the rivers dried up, the flowers died, all medicine became ineffective, and the people waged war out of sheer boredom. Olodumare instructed the deities to apologize to Oshun and, humbly, they did. Satisfied with their supplications, Oshun returned and moistened everything on Earth.

The Family of Isis: Egyptian Isis and Her siblings were born into magic. The old Sun God Ra, whose behavior was often erratic, forbade his children—Geb, the Earth God; and Nut, the Queen of Night—to birth children in any month of His year. But they engaged a magician in a game of chance and won a particle of moonlight. The magician used the light to create five new days. During those days, Nut gave birth to several deities. Isis was born on the first day of the first year of creation. Her birth was followed by Osiris, the Lord of Light; then came Nephthys, the Hidden One; and Set, the Prince of Darkness.

Eventually Isis and Osiris married and brought prosperity to the land. Set became jealous and overpowered His brother through deception, then kidnapped and dismembered Him. Isis roamed all over the world collecting Osiris's pieces. Through another act of magic She reanimated His penis and subsequently gave birth to Horus, the Prince of Light.

Throughout each chapter in this book a very important player must be present—that is you, the reader. The characters in these stories anticipate your embrace. The rituals offered here are designed to connect us to our ancestors, to infuse our celebrations with power and meaning, to strengthen communal ties, and to bring more joy into our lives.

Winter

A Personal Encounter with Winter:
The Night I Swallowed the Moon

In the early 1980s I received, as part of a beautiful ceremony at my home in Oakland, California, a sacred vessel (an *Ikoko Olokun*) for the spirit of the power at the bottom of the Ocean. The ceremony consisted of gathering all the gifts of the Ocean, such as fish, seashells, seaweed, and sand, as well as many gifts of the Earth, such as grains, fruits, vegetables, spices, meat, oil, and eggs. These Ocean gifts and Earth gifts were placed on plates and, intermingled with blue and white candles, lined both sides of a long palm mat. We said prayers of thanksgiving, played drums, sang, and danced while passing the contents of these plates over our heads and around our bodies. We made a commitment to feed the hungry and give all these things back to the Ocean and the Earth at the ceremony's end.

The elders explained to me that there were "greater secrets" to this Ocean ceremony than what I had witnessed and experienced, but they had been lost during the slave period. They also told me that in the Caribbean Islands (Cuba and Puerto Rico, but not Haiti), this force was considered "too powerful" to be fully

Nobody knows what's at the bottom of the Ocean!

—*Yoruba proverb, The Holy Odun Irosun*

ritualized, and, consequently, initiation ceremonies on the islands were not performed for people who dedicated themselves to this layer of the Ocean.

Nine years later I attended an initiation for Olokun in Benin City, Nigeria, where the ritual has remained intact for centuries. The Moonlight ceremony was an event I shall never forget.

The initiate was a man of Latin American descent and a member of my small travel party of five people. The five of us had had high adventure from the moment our plane landed in West Africa. In Dakar, the capital of Senegal, we were met at the airport by lepers—mostly children—who made their living by begging. We survived a taxi ride that resembled a chase scene from an Indiana Jones movie. And, at the hotel, we were greeted by a vulture that took a nosedive into the windowpane of my hotel room. A few days later, after having settled in and then gone lusting after fabric in the Gambia (as part of my travel ritual of purchasing cloth from the countries I visit), we managed to fly across Ghana to Nigeria, eventually arriving in Benin City.

Before this trip, I imagined my part in the proceedings to be that of a mere "go-for." My intention was to deposit the members of my travel party—a daughter of the River at Oshogbo, a son of the thunder in Oyo, a diviner of destiny in Ode Remo, and a child of the deep—at their respective ritual sites, and then I'd go-for food, go-for cloth, and go-for items of personal necessity. I intended to support the others, but I did not intend to participate in any of the rituals myself.

In Benin City, this man of Latin American descent went through the full initiation for Olokun, which consisted of many things yet unknown to me. But, at his request, I was allowed to visit him at the end of his fourteen days of solitude. The officiating priestess housed the initiate in a small room with a floor of pounded earth covered with palm mats. The mats were covered with immaculate white cloth. During my visit, the initiate was covered in *efun* (white chalk) from head to toe—including his eye-balls! He was unfocused, spoke slowly, and said he had been dreaming nonstop for an eternity (although in actuality his non-stop dreaming lasted seven of the fourteen days).

I sat quietly and listened to him talk about his dreams—dreams of being in the Ocean and on the bottom of the Ocean. He spoke of scales, gills, and fins, of movement and colors, and of the smell of

27

salt. I painted pictures in my mind as he spoke. After I had been there awhile, I sneezed. A priestess entered the room carrying a broom made of an herb (I think it was SeaGrape). She promptly cleaned the initiate by sweeping the area around his head and down the outline of his body. Then she swept the corners and the center of the room and threw the broom out the back door of the little room. She informed me that my visit was over, but she invited me to attend the drumming ceremony that was to take place outside the next night.

I arrived at the drumming ceremony late in the evening, my head was covered in a *gele,* a wrap made of white eyelet. I wore the traditional regalia for such a ceremony: white shoes, white dress, white purse. My driver proudly led me to a seat of honor that had been reserved for me. I sat quietly, determined to observe and remember every aspect of the ceremony.

The ritual participants began to gather. As I recall, four drummers came carrying small tub-like drums similar to the East Indian *tabla* but producing a distinctly different sound. The drummers were followed by at least thirty *shekere* (hollowed-out gourds decorated with beads) players—all women—who began immediately to make rushing sounds like the hum of the Ocean with their instruments. The congregation, a cast of hundreds, made a circle around a swept-dirt center. Everyone's body had been painted with white chalk.

After about half an hour, a priestess entered and blew white powder around the circle. She raised her arms as if lifting weights, then pulled them down sharply and leaned left and right as part of the invocation to the four directions. She was establishing the boundaries of sacred space. Once they were established, she let out a high-pitched call, and a procession began. The priestesses who had officiated over the initiation led the procession. They were dressed in red and white garments and hundreds of cowrie shells, the symbols of wealth. Instruments of divination were sewn on their clothes. The initiate was finely dressed in white cloth, and he walked unsteadily in the middle of the procession. The drums started, and the women began to display the initiate and to teach him to dance. I tried to watch the steps.

Eventually, the first priestess walked over to me and blew a handful of white powder directly into my face. Unwillingly I began to tremble from the inside and tears rolled down my cheeks. I became aware of my driver tugging at my purse and shoes. "You must go and dance," he said. I shook my head no in an attempt to clear my blurring vision. "Yes," my driver said, "this thing is happening to you, and you must go and dance now." I wanted to sit and observe, but the priestess returned and blew another handful of powder into my face. Then I whitened out (the opposite of blacking out, I suppose).

I remember a resounding cry and a bolt of energy as if lightning had struck me in my spine. I still have no memory of moving from point A to point B, only of being there in the center of the circle, feeling my legs moving beneath me and my chest and hips gyrating. I heard my own voice above my head ask, "Who is that dancing?" I lifted my eyes to the night sky, then I saw and felt the Full Moon descending into my mouth, squeezing itself down my throat and into my belly.

I became aware that I had been moved to an inner chamber, a place where life-sized figures made of white chalk were somehow painted or inlaid with gold. I looked around, trying to identify the sculptures. I recognized Shango, the God of Thunder, in male and female form, erect and pregnant. Before I could see much more the priestess grabbed my face and pushed my lips forward into a "fish mouth." I knew what this meant, as this is the way I'd been taught to give medicine to babies. With my lips pursed in this manner it was almost impossible to reject the substance now being poured down my throat. Oh, but I tried. Water and leaves, little seashells and grit found their way into my belly.

Then they removed my gele, and again there was a great cry. They called the name of the Thunder deity, because a few days before the women of a distant village had braided my hair in the style worn by devotees of Shango (He is my Father, by the way). I was washed from head to toe; they then smeared me with chalk and drew lines on my face and body. My crisp white eyelet clothing was now streaked with chalk and bits of green leaves. As I looked around me, people moved in the dark, their black faces covered in white chalk, their eyes fully opened, staring at me. I felt as if I were in a Fellini movie or a painted mime drama, and these people seemed to be hovering somewhere between the worlds.

Then the priestesses began making predictions for me. Some of them were worrisome, some of them wonderful. All have proved to be true.

As a result of all these rituals, I feel that my consciousness has been enhanced. My dreams are often prefaced with an image of me running through a house, chased by a great Ocean wave. At the point that I allow the wave to wash over me, my dreams for the night begin. I have found these dreams to be prophetic, symbolic, and instructive. I call them my Benin dreams.

An Introduction to Winter: Blue Mother Moon

Night comes early in Winter. At Moonrise the Earth is quiet, and Nature sleeps beneath Her blanket of snow. She dreams of the coming of Spring, the return of the Sun, a time when She will blush and blossom and birds will sing in Her hair. Tomorrow. Soon. But tonight She embraces the stillness; tonight She exalts the Dark. In the Dreamtime the Blue Mother Moon illuminates the sky. Trees stand shamelessly naked, exposing their branches to the wind. The Moon's light casts deep shadows. Humans gaze at Her in wonder and take refuge in their homes.

There, before the fireplace, we gather. Frosty clouds of breath escape from our mouths. Reverently we lay oak logs and strike a match in honor of the Sun. And comforted, we warm our hands as Blue Mother Moon smiles. We gather our family around us, embrace friends, and make peace with our enemies. We cook

31

life-sustaining porridge and bake breads made of wheat, oats, and rye. Those who can afford it will flock to warm climates, to Florida or Jamaica, to bask in the Sun. The unfortunate ones, the homeless people, will wander in the streets. They will freeze, starve, and die, and Blue Mother Moon will cry for Her children.

The truly fortunate, who possess a kind heart, will open their doors and their pockets. Soup kitchens will flourish, and the sad eyes of needy children will be brightened by holiday gifts sincerely given. Through mutual help we will survive the Winter.

The Winter Solstice

The symbols of Christmas—the Nativity scene, the tree with its lights, the gift giving, and nearly all the songs of the season—have their roots in the pre-Christian tradition of the Winter Solstice.

The Wheel of the Year charts the movement of the Sun. The Winter Solstice (December 21) is the longest night and the shortest day of the year. Now, when the Sun is at its weakest point (in the astrological sign of Capricorn), humans turn inward to sleep and dream (just as Demeter weeps for the lost Persephone). We make appeals to the Sun to return to us, to bring us through Winter's Darkness into the Light of Spring. We make these appeals in the symbolic language of myths and rituals by creating celebrations of Light that reflect our hopes and dreams. Some of these celebrations begin in the darkest part of Autumn, before the Solstice, and continue throughout the Winter season. From the point of the Solstice onward, the Sun increases in strength, and we declare that "He (the Son of the Sun) is born" from the virginal womb of the Great Dark Mother.

The Sun represents the male God, and its death and rebirth on the Winter Solstice is seen as the death of the old solar year and the birth of the new, or the birth of the Divine Child, the Sun God of the new solar year. To the Egyptians he was Horus, the Divine child of Isis and Osiris; to the Greeks and Romans he was Apollo, son of Zeus and twin brother to Artemis, the Goddess of the Moon; to Norse and Anglo-Saxons he was Balder; to the Phoenicians, Baal; and to the Celts, Bel.[1]

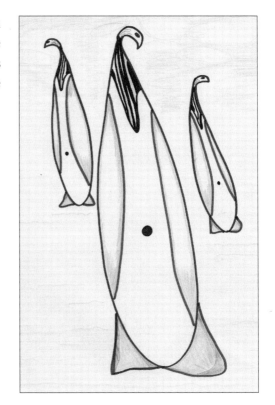

Bring us through Winter's darkness into the light of Spring.

The Christmas Tree symbolizes the Tree of Life, and the traditional holiday wreath and Yule log both represent the Wheel of the Year, the travels of the Sun. They are evergreens, plants that maintain their powers in winter; they are decorated with symbols of increase, plenty, and light. *Tannenbaum,* from the popular song "Oh Tannenbaum," which is sung when the tree is lit, is a Celtic word that means "sacred tree," and *yule* is a German word that means "the wheel."

The ancient roots of Christmas become even clearer when we consider the Roman holiday of Saturnalia (December 17–24). During this time the rules of society were relaxed and social positions were reversed. The king became a pauper, masters served their servants, and little dolls were given as gifts in honor of Oops, the Goddess of Opulence. December 24 was the Night of the Mothers, when the power of birthing was celebrated. (At one time the church declared this Adam and Eve Night.) On this night women were exalted for their ability to produce and nurture human life. (Later we will explore the celebrations of the Mother Goddess that occur this time of year in Brazil and West Africa.) The next day, December 25, was Juvenalia, Children's Day, when the youngsters were given wonderful food and warm things to wear, especially socks, which became the present-day Christmas stocking. It seems the mothers of my childhood retained this custom, whether they knew its origins or not. Giving warm clothing is a practice I'd like to see reembraced during the time of the Winter holidays.

The practice of kissing under the mistletoe gets risky—depending upon who is in the room! This covert courtship ritual comes from the Druids, who saw symbols of fertility in this evergreen plant with white berries (semen) and golden roots (sunlight).

At midnight on December 31 our ancestors made great noises to chase away the Spirits of the old year. Sometimes a doll made of old clothes was buried at midnight. Today Old Father Time, who is bearded, robed, and carrying a blade, yields to a bouncing baby boy wearing a crisp new diaper, blowing a horn, and throwing confetti, and everybody cries out joyously, "Happy New Year." The old pagan rituals live on in Christian clothing.

And in the second half of the twentieth century, the African American holiday of Kwanzaa was born, and the cycle of new traditions birthing from old lives on.

Christmas

The story of Christmas is probably the most well-known myth of origin in Western culture. The short version goes like this:

> Mary, the daughter of Anne and Joachim, was a virgin. The Angel Gabriel visited her and informed her that she would be "overshadowed" by a dove. God, her Father, who made her without the Original Sin of Eve, would impregnate her (by blowing in her ear) so that she could give birth to Him as her son. Her widowed fiancé, Joseph, agreed to the plan without question. But they had to deal with the government like everybody else, so they went to Bethlehem to register for the census. While there, she gave birth to a baby boy in a stable. Three wise men (one of them Black) followed a star from a great distance to come visit the child, who was born on December

25 (an arbitrary date). That was the first Christmas. His birth gave the Western world its division of historical time. From then on, Western history would be measured as occurring before (B.C. and backward) or after (A.D. and forward) the birth of her little boy, the illustrious ancestor supported by and identified with or as God.

—*Luisah Teish*

Celebrants recount the story by constructing a nativity scene with Mother, Father, Child, and Visitors all in their places on the front lawn. Their homes are adorned with beautifully colored lights, and Yule logs crackle in the fireplace. They decorate a green tree with delicate glass bulbs, hovering angels, drizzling snow, candy canes, and on the very top a guiding light . . . a star. Songs are sung, a delicious meal is consumed, and people kiss under the mistletoe. When the glowing embers of the Yule log turn to ashes, and as children sleep through the midnight hour, the Flying Dutchman arrives.

Santa Claus: The Flying Dutchman

Santa Claus is an American adaptation of Sint Nikolaas (Saint Nicholas), the Flying Dutchman. He is also known as Père Noël, Grandfather Frost, and Kris Kringle. He is believed to have been a bishop from Anatolia who wore a red suit trimmed in white fur. His flying reindeers, Rudolph and Company, may have come from Scandinavia. In Northern and Eastern Europe, the feast of Saint

Nicholas, known for the generous tossing of sacks of money through the windows of poor homes, was celebrated on December 5 or 6.

The American Santa Claus is more of a secular folk character than a sacred one. He is "saintly" in that he judges the behavior of children ("He's making a list, checking it twice, gonna find out who's naughty or nice") and rewards good behavior with toys and sweets.

A Black Christmas

I am a country girl at heart and usually spend most of my time in the countryside outside of whatever city I visit. I guess you could call my need for the country an "Earth Jones." I just have to be in the greens. When traveling I always buy a piece of cloth indigenous to the area and a book of the regional folklore so that I can take a piece of the "real people" home with me.

I'd been in Holland a few weeks one November and needed another travel bag to accommodate the books and clothes I'd bought and the gifts I'd been given. Until this day I'd spent most of my time in the countryside, but I was coming to love the city of Amsterdam with its waterways and tulip gardens and free spirit. I was enchanted by the statues of Hermes and Poseidon overlooking the canals, seduced by vendors selling cheese and Belgian lace, and flattered by an occasional flirtatious smile. I found the sugar beets, windmills, and old castles intriguing. I still wasn't accustomed to the flatlands of Amsterdam and all of Holland (the source of the name "the Netherlands"), and I did find myself missing the beautiful hills of the San Francisco Bay Area.

My companions agreed to escort me through the major department stores in Amsterdam. We turned a corner and suddenly I was confronted by Dutch Christmas decorations. (The sight of Christmas decorations in November has always irritated me. The effort to project a Winter holiday into the Fall season feels *unnatural* to me. In the United States some stores begin their Christmas advertising as early as the day after Halloween! The rush to the mall (spell that m-a-w-l) and its buying frenzy makes me dizzy. It is, for me, "the nightmare before Christmas.")

As I walked with my friends from one store to the next, I became aware of the presence of a Black figure in holiday decorations. I'd met many Black people from Suriname living in Holland, but this figure did not reflect any of that culture. Some displays depicted a stylish Black high-fashion mannequin, whereas others used the image of a pollywog—a bug-eyed black doll with big white or red lips. These made me think of black-faced minstrels. In the minstrel shows of the American theater, White men put burnt cork on their faces and acted out outrageous stereotypes of Black people. In these shows Blacks were always depicted as lazy, fearful, and ignorant. In the post-slavery period, when African American performers sought the stage, they were forced to blacken their natural faces and perform an imitation of an imitation of themselves.

Curious and a bit insulted, I began taking pictures of the Black figure. Eventually my companions noticed my interest and unrest and introduced me to this character. His name is Black Peter, and he's Santa Claus' hit man. At first I thought they were pulling my leg, but a little research confirmed this piece of information.

> In much of Europe, and particularly in Holland, the main fun takes place on St. Nicholas Eve, December 5. According to the story, St. Nicholas, who was a Bishop, comes each year in a ship from Spain, riding a white horse, to visit every child. To those who are good he will give a gift of sweets or biscuits, and those who have been bad get a light smack with a bunch of birch twigs. Children set out a clog or shoe beside the fireplace containing some hay, bread, and a carrot to reward the saint's horse, in the hope that his assistant, Black Pete, will leave a present, rather than delivering a smack or, worse still, wrapping the really bad children up in the empty sack he carries and transporting them away to Spain as captives.[2]

I found this character interesting but also disturbing.

In Europe and the United States, Christmas is a time of drama, music, and pageantry. The *Nutcracker* ballet and the Mummers' plays are performed in this season. Traditionally, the Mummers' theme is a battle between a White Knight and a Black Villain, usually depicted as being of Turkish (Moslem) or Moorish descent. Of course, the White Knight always wins. I ponder whether this is a reenactment of the "battle between Day and Night," or is it an emotional response to the Moorish conquest dramatized? In any event, I am not enamored of this holiday as it is celebrated in popular American culture.

I have attended Christmas parties where a Black man shows up as Santa Claus. Sometimes this works for the children, whose imaginations allow them to accept the essence of the folk character without knowledge of the true history. But it just doesn't work for me personally. And, as we shall see later, many African Americans have made the choice to celebrate Kwanzaa instead of, or in addition to, some of the Eurocentric festivities like the one described previously.

The Meaning and Joy of Christmas

Many times I have seen children who are disappointed because "Santa" did not leave them a disco Barbie Doll or that plastic helicopter that cost $39.95 and is guaranteed *not* to fly. I've also tried to assuage the pain and frustration of hard-working, well-meaning parents who feared losing the respect and affection of their disappointed children. And I've seen other families where expensive gifts are given in lieu of love.

The humility, warmth, and joy of the original Holy Family and their Visitors are what this season is all about. At the end of this chapter I will share information that anyone, of any ethnicity, income level, or location, can use to create meaningful and joyous celebrations for family and friends.

Kwanzaa

Maulana Ron Karenga, a Black Studies professor at California State University, Long Beach, configured the African and American holiday known as Kwanzaa in 1966. The word *Kwanzaa* means "First Fruit" in the Swahili language of East Africa. But the practices of giving thanks for the harvest are observed all over Africa and indeed around the world. Kwanzaa has developed as a cultural celebration and may be observed by people of African descent in lieu of or in addition to any other practices (Christmas, Ramadan, whatever). It was designed to reinforce some basic African values, to revere the ancestors, and to strengthen cultural unity.

The Kwanzaa celebration begins on December 26 and ends on January 1. Each night, the community gathers before an altar, which is dressed with the symbols of the season: a mat, an ear of corn and other produce, a unity cup, the African American flag (which is red, black, and green), homemade gifts, a poster, and a candle holder. The candle holder, known as the Kinara, accommodates seven tapered lights. The candles, like the flag, are red (the blood), black (the people), and green (the land). Each night, a candle is lit for one of the Seven Principles of Kwanzaa, the Nguzo Saba. The seven principles are

1. Umoja (unity)
2. Kujichagulia (self-determination)
3. Ujima (collective work)
4. Ujamaa (shared economics)

5. Nia (life purpose)

6. Kuumba (creativity)

7. Imani (faith)

The principles of Kwanzaa when earnestly practiced reflect the same life-preserving values to which every culture aspires. In the Kwanzaa celebration the cultural notions made on Universal Principles are consciously and specifically African. This does not mean that the celebration is closed to non-Africans. Rather it means that the focus must remain on the contributions and values of African people, and that those who officiate over the ceremony should be devotees and elders of the culture. Everyone else is considered an invited guest.

I began celebrating Kwanzaa in 1968. I served as a Name Giver. Whenever community members wanted to reclaim their ancestors by taking an African name, I was pleased to help with the selection, to calculate the effect of its meaning, and to proclaim it to the community, usually on the night of self-determination.

For decades, families and small communities of people celebrated Kwanzaa almost as if it were an underground institution. Since 1995 Kwanzaa has made its way into the popular media. I would like to believe that the values of Kwanzaa and the contributions of African culture have come to the public's attention; however, I fear that this new popularity and acceptance is more a function of commodity culture, the work of corporate commercialism.

The gifts given at Kwanzaa should be homemade, or handmade by community artists, and not from factories made by slave labor. Beside the gifts of kinship, culture, and food, a book is prescribed as a symbol of our respect for learning. Everyone may share in the joy of the season—we can all dance to the drum. But the most important gift is the preservation of the cultural identity of the children. (For more information about this holiday, I can recommend the Web site *www.officialkwanzaawebsite.org/celebrating.html*.)

The Celebration of Bembe Elegba

Elegba, the Master of the Crossroads, is celebrated on New Year's Day in Cuba, Caracas, Venezuela, and Oakland, California. At this time the diviners cast palm nuts, kola nuts, coins, and cowrie shells to read the messages of the deities. We ask the oracle what natural occurrences (earthquakes, heat waves, firestorms, or floods) and what human tendencies (fear, violence, compassion, or creativity) are most likely to manifest in the coming year. We ask what the deities have in store for us, and we ask how we should conduct ourselves.

Divination may be done for individuals, groups, or the entire world. From these castings, predictions are made and the diviner prescribes rituals to be performed throughout the year to receive blessings and avert danger. Offerings are made and the drums are played and the people dance and rejoice.

But Elegba, the Trickster, reminds us that Time is a matter of perception. And so we say "Happy New Year" as more of a joke,

43

Winter

because we know that the year isn't really new until the palm branches blossom in Spring.

Winter Celebrations in the African Diaspora

In the African diaspora (the spread of African traditions throughout the world), the Great Waters are celebrated many times and in many ways. The most popular celebrations occur between December 21 and 31.

> Night comes early in Winter; the Dark is deep and long. Yet in the stillness of sleep and death, Yemaya gives us Her song. In Her quiet dreaming the hum of the Ocean is heard. In the rushing waters Olokun gives us the Word. I was there in the beginning. And I'll be there until the end. In my depths new life is teeming. All that dies shall live again.

Yemaya, Yemonja, Imanje—the Mother of the Night—is worshiped in Africa, Brazil, the Caribbean, and the United States. Those of us whose ancestors survived the treacherous middle passage of the slavery holocaust pay homage to Her as Our Mother and Protectress.

In my lifetime I have stood on the seaboard side of the Last Door on Goree Island. Goree Island, located off the coast of Senegal, West Africa, was a warehouse and shipping dock for slave sellers and slave ships. The members of my party and I walked through the fort as our guide described the enslavement process to us. We could still hear the chains rattling and smell the blood-soaked earth. He took us to the Rape Room, where African women were sadistically raped by the ship's crew while African men, bound and gagged, were forced to watch. I felt my nostrils flare open; another woman in my party began to shake and cry. We had to leave that room quickly. As we were walking away I saw myself crouched in a small cell in the wall. I stopped suddenly and stared at it. My guide informed me that this was a punishment cell, where they put slaves who revolted or tried to run away. He ended by saying, "Ah, my sister, you remember too much." I will never forget that moment. We walked through the Last Door, our hands untied, with no chains on our feet. We looked out over the water and remembered the millions of ancestors who were thrown or who jumped into the Ocean during the long journey into the Unknown Darkness of the Future. And there, with salt water lapping at our feet, we performed a ritual giving thanks for having survived the ordeal, asking that the door be sealed, and dedicating our lives to the struggle for freedom for all people. We were a mixed party of Black, White, and Brown people, but we all understood where we were and how we'd come to be there.

Because the waters of the Ocean touch the shores of every continent and surround the Islands of the world, Yemaya (by whatever name we call Her) is recognized as the Eternal Mother who gives birth, nurtures Life, and protects us all. Yoruba mythology says that Yemonja and Her brother/husband, Aganju, are the first set of twins

45

born of Obatala (the White Clouds) and Oduddua (the Black Goddess of the Earth and the twin sister of Olorun). Aganju, the Lord of the Wilderness, is sometimes associated with the Volcano. Together, Yemonja and Aganju are Water and Land. When a volcano erupts and the lava flows to the Sea, it cools there and new land is born. It is said that Yemonja and Aganju mated and gave birth to Orungan, the height of the sky. The myth says that Orungan, however, had no twin sister, and so He pursued His mother as a mate. Yemonja was not pleased by His attentions and fled. As She ran across the face of the Earth, She fell backward and Her belly burst open, spreading rivers, lakes, and streams everywhere and giving birth to a host of deities. She carries on flirtations with Ogun, the Wildman, in the Woods as the edge of the Forest meets the Ocean's shore, and Her waves splash against the rocks.

Yemonja is also closely associated with Olokun, the God of the Sea. Olokun is envisioned as a Black man with long flowing hair and mudfish legs. Legend associates Him with a king who was paralyzed. He dresses royally in coral and seashells and lives in a palace at the bottom of the Sea. In Haiti, He is known as Agwe Taroyo. Together, Yemonja and Olokun are the salt waters of the Earth, the weight of the planet, the substance from which the clouds are made. Their domain is rich and wondrous, populated by mystical beings who work with them to maintain the world of the Deep. There is Elusu, the chalk-white Mermaid, and Olosa, the Lady of the Lagoon. There is Erinle, the medicines found in the Ocean, and Odima, who is associated with lost treasure that sunk at Sea.

There is also Mami Wata and Her husband Papa Densu.

In Brazil Yemonja is known as Imanje, an alluring Mermaid of great popularity. Many of the sambas that are danced in the Carnival Jump Up are written and played for Her. And, as we shall see, She owns the beach at Rio de Janiero.

In Cuban mythology, Yemaya is both the Sacred Portal of Birth and the One who gave us the First Hole for burial. Clearly, she is the Mother of Mystery.

Yemaya is the Ocean Herself, the Primal Intelligence that existed on the planet in its Winter, before Life developed in the Garden.

The Great Waters are celebrated throughout Africa and the lands Africa has touched, most deeply during the Winter season.

Celebrating the Deep

Pick up your rattle

Pack up your dreams

Dress yourself in fine whites

We'll walk hand in hand

In a magical land

That exists between

Twilight and Night.

There on the seashore

We'll knock on the door

Of the Mother of

Darkness and Light.
We'll enter the Deep
There we'll dream
As we sleep
And behold Her
A wondrous sight!
—*Luisah Teish*

The Feast of Mami Wata

Mami Wata and Her husband, Densu, are revered in Togo and Ghana. She is envisioned as a chalk-white Mermaid who carries a golden dagger and a trident. Her husband is a paisley-eyed, dark-haired gentleman from India.

African spirituality (like most indigenous traditions) is, by nature, embracing and integrative. It tends to identify similarities, accept what works, and integrate seemingly disparate elements. Many of the traditions of the African diaspora reflect complex mixtures: the original culture, the colonizers' culture, and that of other people imported to the area. So, Papa Densu came from India and found a home in Africa.

Deities reflect a people's ideas and beliefs about the laws of nature as expressed through their experience of the environment and each other. Often people who live near the Ocean will populate their world with Mer-creatures—some of them are pale because they reside at the very bottom of the Sea where, we assume, the Sun does not shine. On the other hand, a proverb of the neighboring Yoruba people says, "Nobody knows what's at the bottom of the Ocean," and their water spirits are varying colors born out of black.

The worshipers of Mami Wata are predominately women, though there are men who participate in Her worship. The priestesses of Mami Wata are called "Mamissi"; they are often childless and participate in the Great Power of the Mother through their devotion to the Mermaid.

A woman is called to the service of Mami Wata through dreams. The Mermaid appears in the dream with Her snakes and calls the person to initiation. The Feast of Mami Wata, celebrated on December 21, marks the end of the year and the anticipation of the new season. Old relics are stored away, and the new ones are introduced. The ceremony for Mami Wata begins with a procession of musicians, dancers, and devotees who have painted their bodies with white chalk. It is very similar to the ceremony I described earlier in Benin City, Nigeria, on the night I swallowed the moon. After dancing in trance for a period of time, there is a procession to the beach. The Mamissi carry offerings for the Goddess down to the sea. There they stand in the surf and meditate, awaiting the call of the Mermaid. Perhaps it is the curve of a wave or a figure seen in the mist. Perhaps it is a reflection of light on the water or the whisper of shifting sand. But something is perceived, and the mystery unfolds. The women hear the call of the Mermaid and are pulled by the tide of the Ocean. They throw

49

themselves into the Ocean; by the hundreds they plunge into the salty waters of the Great Womb. They pray for Power, for Vision, for Oneness with the Mother. They lose themselves in the vastness of the Sea. Many of the women cannot swim and are caught in the rhythm of the water. Now young men (who are fully dressed) dive into the Sea and save them from the call of the dangerous Goddess.

Celebrations of the Waters in the West

Many aspects of the celebrations for Yemaya and Olokun, Mami Wata, and Papa Densu have been preserved by their devotees living in the Western Hemisphere.

In Brazil, Imanje (Yemonja's name there) is celebrated on New Year's Eve. Literally millions of people dressed in dazzling white clothes process down to the beaches of Rio de Janeiro and Bahia carrying little boats made of banana and palm leaves, loaded with offerings of fruit, mirrors, and money. Drums are played, songs are sung, and dancing goes on deep into the night. When the sky is at its darkest, the people entreat the Great Goddess to come and take their offerings and to give them a sign of the promise of a better year. And without fail it happens! At midnight a great wave sweeps up on the shore, swallowing the offerings, scooping them in Her arms, and taking them out to sea. There is a great burst of music and song. The coastline rocks as the people jump for joy until sunrise. There are fires on the beach, good food, and lovemaking. And like the devotees of Mami Wata, some of the participants leap into the sea. The same celebration is performed for Agwe Taroyo in Haiti (Olokun's name on that island) and I dare say for the Great Waters all over the world.

Back in the "before time," in the darkness, Intelligence mated with Power. And in Her pregnant belly the single cell evolved, creating seaweed, hydra, and fish. All the Power that was, that is, that ever shall be, is there waiting for you to dream it, to bring it forth from the potentiality of Winter to the blossoming reality of Spring. Sleep, and in that sleeping, wake. Go into the darkness, and once there, see the light. It is the shining eye of the serpent Damballah Hwedo. He knows the secrets, all that has been thought and felt. All that has been lost is found in the glimmer of His eyes.

Suggestions for Celebrating Winter

As I share these little tidbits and make suggestions for celebrating Winter, I am envisioning a group of women, men, and children who know each other relatively well, who enjoy each other's company, and who want to create a celebration for the season. The recommendations made here are similar to the practices of my own extended family.

The Great Mother Tree of Life

The tree can be anything that is still green during your Winter season. This may mean the traditional Christmas Tree, the Douglas

Fir, a tree in your front or back yard, or your favorite potted houseplant. I much prefer a living tree of some kind to one that has been cut off from its life source, and personally I just can't envision decorating an aluminum tree. The most important aspect of the tree is its representation of the promise of the return of the Sun (renewal) and the anticipation of joy (hope). So you will want to decorate this Tree of Life with those things that symbolize this hope and promise.

At my home we honor the Great Mother Tree of Life by decorating it with globes of hope and light. We use several packages of inexpensive bulbs, the kind that are Styrofoam balls wrapped in silkened thread. Sometimes all the bulbs are one color, and other times they are a rainbow of colors. Using fabric paint, the kind that comes in small tube-like squeeze bottles, we inscribe our hopes on them in Yoruba, English, and Spanish. We use single words such as *Ache* (Power), *Ire* (Good Fortune), *Owo* (Money), and *Alafia* (Health) and hang them on the tree. These requests are made for ourselves and for other individuals. We inscribe Healing for sick friends and Friendship for those who are lonely. And we take into account the needs of nations as well. We ask for LaPaz (for wartorn countries), Independencia (Independence), and Salud (Health).

We also inscribe these circles of light with the names of the Orishas of the Yoruba pantheon, the Loa of Haiti, the Neters of Egypt, and other world deities of the season.

So you will find on our tree red and black crossmarks for Elegba, the Master of the Crossroads; blue silkened balls for Yemaya-

Olokun and the finned creatures; bright red fireballs for Shango, the Lord of the Flame; shiny white balls for Obatala, the Cloud King; gold and silver ornaments for Isis and Osiris, Lady and Lord of Light; and some multicolored wavy lines wrapped around the world for Damballah and Aida Hwedo, the Rainbow Serpents.

I have ornaments for the Sun, Moon, and Stars, the mythological creatures (mermaids and unicorns), the fruit and flowers, and a host of ancestors. The process for making these ornaments is very simple. Get a sheet of poster or construction paper, cut the paper in the appropriate shape (circle, square, triangle), copy an image or cut one out from a magazine or draw an original one, and paste the image onto the paper. Then use a single-hole paper punch to place a hole in the figure (usually top and center), and run a piece of yarn through the hole. Tie it securely but lightly, and then tie it onto the tree.

You may want to put the Sun, Moon, and Stars on the top of the tree, and below them the Deities intermingled with plants, animals, and human images. And of course the things of the Sea may be placed at the bottom of the tree. Let your intuition guide you through this process. Allow the kids to make some creatures and place them on the tree. Then string the tree with the lights of your choice and other decorations that have meaning for you.

The Seasonal Altar

If you are fortunate enough to have a space in your home that can accommodate a seasonal altar, you may want to create one that will remain intact throughout the season (until January 2 or even March 20).

For the seasonal altar, I recommend a color scheme that reflects the energy you want to embody for the season. For example, if you regard Christmas as the major holiday of the year, then the altar will reflect that preference. The cloth will be a traditional Christmas pattern of white, red, and green. Some people have holiday dishes in these colors with pictures of Christmas Trees or people riding in the snow.

If you prefer to celebrate the season of "the Mothers" and the "Divine Child," you may want to dedicate the altar to a deity such as Yemaya-Olokun. In that instance I recommend an altar cloth of satiny deep blue for the night Sky, luminescent silver for the Moon, and seaweed green for the fertility of the Ocean. This altar can be decorated with seashells and mirrors and other things that dreams are made of. You may also want to place a bowl of salt water (with blue food coloring and a candle in it) in the center of the altar area.

The Seasonal Table

Like the altar, the Holiday dinner table should reflect all the things that you consider holy. It should have light and water, flowers and food. I take great pleasure in creating a beautiful holiday table and sometimes have a special flower arrangement created of a miniature oak log, holly berries, and an assortment of flowers. The table setting below illustrates a blend of a seasonal altar and dining table setting. Sometimes I use:

A maroon-colored tablecloth

A gold place setting shaped like a scallop shell

A green bayberry candle in a glass or a dramatically tall one, if available

A statue representing the Goddess Yemaya (in a bowl of sand surrounded by seashells)

Several bright red Poinsettias (on another small table nearby)

Bowls of nuts, cookies, and candies placed nearby

The scent of potpourri fills the room. I stand there grinning from ear to ear, so proud of my artistic ability. Everyone agrees that I've done a wonderful job; sometimes they even clap and take pictures. It's both reverent and beautiful, but, truthfully, it doesn't last long in my household because it is usually overwhelmed by the presence of the food. Soon we move the decorations to another table and clear the way for an ethnic feast to match our Spirits. We bring on the gumbo, the big bird, and the cornbread.

A Winter Ritual

This ritual can be performed at any time during the Winter season.

Preparations

For this ritual you will need these items:

A recording of sounds of the Ocean

Clothing that reflects the colors of the Sea

A mat

Objects from the Sea and/or those associated with the qualities of the Sea (seashells, coral, silver objects, Moonshapes, and mirrors)

A seven-day deep-blue candle in a glass

A seven-day green candle in a glass

A large bowl with blue water in it

Blessed anointing oil (I recommend Meditation or Sweet Dreams oil)

Small musical instruments

Seven dimes

A folk or fairy tale about Mer-people or Ocean creatures

Songs and food to share

Smudge in a seashell

A silver bell

Clean and decorate the room. Play the Ocean tape and allow the sound of the Sea to fill the room before the ritual begins.

Altar Building: This ritual may be performed in front of the seasonal altar described in the previous section ("The Seasonal Altar"). It could also be done in the presence of the dinner table; however, because people are so drawn by the power of food, I recommend that the ritual be performed in another room, away from the dinner table, or shortened to allow for the appetites of family and friends.

Entry: As the participants (hereafter referred to as "family") enter the room, they may place their ritual objects on the altar table or mat. Choose a comfortable place to sit. (I recommend a comfortable chair or pillows on the floor with room to lie down.) Listen to the sounds of the Ocean and be quiet.

Smudge: The oldest woman in the house (or She Who Has the Most Children) should mix a smudge of sage, rosemary, hyssop, and lemon verbena and smudge the altars and the people. As she does this, moving West, North, East, and South, the youngest woman in the house (or She Who Has No Children) should follow her, ringing a silver bell.

Invocation to the Directions

Center: Face the altar. Invoke the power of the Trickster. Visualize yourself as the spark of all beginnings. Ask for the power to truly change your life in the coming year.

West: Turn and face the West. Invoke the powers of the West and the Western ancestors. Ask for a beautiful interior life, for sweet dreams and loving family. Ask for the health and protection of women and children and for better understanding between women and men in the coming year.

North: Turn and face the North. Invoke the powers of the North and the Northern ancestors (the Europeans and/or whatever people inhabit the land north of where you are). Ask for the power of manifestation and the preservation of the Earth in the coming year.

57

Winter

East: Turn and face the East. Invoke the powers of the East and the Eastern ancestors. Ask for inspiration and the peaceful use of technology in the coming year.

South: Turn and face the South. Invoke the powers of the South and the Southern ancestors. Ask for personal courage, for the healing of sexually transmitted disease, the end of sexual abuse, and the cooling of international temperaments in the coming year.

If this ritual is a group effort, the invocation to the directions can be shared by five people. Choose one person to hold the center. The other four people will stand facing their respective directions and remain there until all the directions have been invoked. At the end of the invocation, everyone will return to the center.

Performing the Ritual

Deep-Sea Chant: Hand in hand, with eyes closed, the family takes seven slow, deep breaths, breathing in the sound and feel of the Ocean's depth. Now family members call out the names of Sea deities (Goddesses and Gods) and chant these names. Play with the names, stretch the vowels, hammer the consonants, allow them to crescendo and decrescendo into a cacophony of sound. Return to silence. Listen to the sounds of the Ocean. Melt down into your seats, lie down on the floor, relax in Yemaya's arms.

Guided Visualization: A visualization should be spoken by

someone who has a soothing voice. The sounds of the Ocean create the background music; occasionally the tinkle of the maiden's silver bell is heard. Light the blue candle. The visualization should take the family back to Mother's womb, to the depths of the Ocean. It should speak to the creative and regenerative powers of Mother's womb and Father's seed. Family members are encouraged to recreate themselves, to compose a new person for the New Year. This visualization works best when it is delivered impromptu (this preserves the virginity of it). If you prefer to read it from a prepared script, let your voice be influenced by the rhythm of the Ocean. The speaker should visually walk into the Ocean, experience *de*volution and union with Her other life forms, return to a single cell, and recreate herself. If you are the speaker, speak the directives that will seduce others into similar feelings as you are experiencing this recreation. In this way the speaker will remain part of the flow. Let your own words come through as you speak.

The Recovery: As the visualization ends, the family will open their eyes and sit up. Now it is time to share the experiences from the Ocean bottom. Members will volunteer to share their stories. Anyone who wishes to remain silent may do so. Invite family members to choose a name or title for themselves that bespeaks their experience, for example, Seaweed Woman, Green Dolphin Queen, Aqua Marine.

Anointing: Now pass the anointing oil around the circle. Each person should anoint her or his third eye (between the eyebrows), heart (between the breasts), and navel while pronouncing their sacred name. Some people may want to use this name throughout the year. If the name is that of a sea creature, it may be used as a dream totem. Ask your personal wisdom if this totem is your dream companion for the year.

Make Merry: After the anointing, members may pick up their small instruments and create a "makeshift orchestra." Begin with a steady drumbeat, something soft and comforting. Let instruments join in at will. Build the music up. Get up and move your body. Swim through the space, flip-flop, and dive through the air. Each person should only stop playing and dancing when they are ready. Decrease the music and the movement until there is only the sound of the drum, the silver bell, and the Ocean in the background.

The Mother of Secrets: Each person will bring out their seven dimes. Whisper your hopes, dreams, and aspirations to the seven dimes. Take your time. Be clear. When you are ready, go to the bowl of blue water. Say, "All powerful, all healing, most beautiful Mother, give birth," and drop the dimes in the Ocean.

Each person will dip their hands in the water, just enough to carry a wet hand over to their ritual object on the altar mat. Sprinkle your ritual object with Ocean water, pick it up, and return to your seat.

At this point a woman should deliver an Oriki (praise-poem) in honor of the Ocean. A few words will do. Simply share a personal story about the beauty and power of the Ocean, or confess how much you love Her, thank Her for Her undying dance, Her endless nurturing.

Close the Directions: Lightly or firmly dismiss the directions South, East, North, and West. To extinguish the candles simply pinch the flames with moistened fingers. Do not blow the candles out. Share food, conversation, and song. Read a folktale. Play like children.

A Winter Recipe: Teish's Creole Combo

Holiday dinners are a time for conspicuous displays of the art of cooking. Everyone can have the opportunity to show off their ability to produce old favorites such as turkey and dressing and to introduce new and exotic recipes from the latest cookbook or their ancestral culture.

A seafood soup is appropriate as a tribute to Yemaya-Olokun. The Mother of the Children of the Sea offers us a great variety of good things to eat. You may make or purchase cioppino, bouillabaisse, clam chowder, crab, lobster, or conch bisque. Almost any fish soup will scent the air deliciously and warm the bellies of your guests. Vegetarians may want to use tempeh and seaweed for their soup.

Being from New Orleans, I am biased in favor of seafood gumbo. But gumbo is serious business where I come from. It is a universal favorite, it has regional peculiarities, and everyone swears that their personal recipe is the absolute best. For example, on the issue of the roux (the browned flour gravy that goes in the soup), some people want it "well oiled," while others prefer "fat free." On the West Bank of the Mississippi River, where I grew up, many cooks put whole tomatoes in the gumbo (my personal preference) in addition to the roux, and others add whole kernel corn to the soup. Cooks may argue bitterly over this or that point of taste. The name *gumbo* is an African word meaning "okra," a vegetable that I personally cannot stand. Once I had a loud argument with an Igbo man who declared that if I omitted the okra, the dish I was cooking could not be called gumbo. So, instead I call it my Creole Combo. On both sides of the river, across the Sea, and through the bush, we all agree on one thing: The soup must be spicy and consumed with joy.

My mother and I used to spend days and nights shopping and chopping, baking and basting, laughing and crying (while peeling onions) as we cooked the holiday meal. Let me tell you, honey, in my kitchen things have changed. Now I have food processors, seasonings and sauces prepackaged from health food stores and gourmet restaurants, and fancy space-age pots that can cook a meal in 15 minutes. I've learned to open a bag, unscrew a jar, adjust the pressure, and do a thousand other things while the food cooks. Unless I am trying a brand new recipe, I rarely measure anything anymore. But please don't tell my mother.

Ingredients

   1 large yellow onion

   1 medium green bell pepper

   ¼ teaspoon cayenne pepper

   A few stalks of celery

   1 large can of whole tomatoes

   2 cups chicken broth

   2 tablespoons flour

   Water

   2 teaspoons Creole spice blend

   Cooking oil (I use Canola)

   Your favorite chicken parts, cut into bit-sized pieces (bone in for extra flavor)

   1 pound jumbo prawns

   Your favorite sausage (I use turkey smoked sausage)

   6–12 crab claws

   Dash of gumbo filé

Cooking Instructions

Cut the smoked sausage into medium-sized rounds. Place the sausage and the chicken pieces in a pan, and fry just enough to render the fat.

Chop up the onions, bell pepper, and celery, then sauté them in the remaining fat. Transfer this mixture to your soup pot.

Now add just a little oil to the frying pan and heat it.

Then carefully sprinkle the flour into the oil while stirring constantly.

Let the flour brown (according to how brown/thick you want the soup).

Turn the fire down and pour in at least 1 cup of water, stirring constantly to eliminate lumps and for safety's sake.

This will make beautiful brown gravy. Pour this into the soup pot.

Add the chicken broth, the can of whole tomatoes, and the Creole spice (or a crab boil bag if you prefer).

Let this mixture cook on medium heat for 50 to 60 minutes.

Add the crab and cook for another 30 minutes over medium heat (assuming you have conventional cooking pots).

Now toss in the prawns, reduce the heat, and let this soup simmer for another 20 to 30 minutes.

Turn the heat off and add a teaspoon of gumbo filé. Stir.

Let stand until ready to serve.

Cook some white rice.

Make some cornbread.

Serve with salad, the big bird, and your favorite vegetables.

This last step is very important: Call me up and invite me to dinner.

Spring

A Personal Encounter with Spring: C'mon Baby, Let the Good Times Roll

Laissez les bontemps rouler. "Let the good times roll" is a popular New Orleans expression. Although one hears it primarily at Mardi Gras, it may be uttered anytime a Jump Up is in process. I will never forget the feeling that permeated the city at Mardi Gras during my childhood (the late '50s). Excitement is an understatement. People were very busy making costumes, cooking, and planning which parades they would participate in. There was the body-to-body contact of the crowded streets, the flying confetti, and the popular cry, "Throw me something, mister." Mister was anybody riding a Carnival float, and the something was usually strings of brightly colored beads, although occasionally a coconut. After the festivities, we children would barter and bargain with each other, trading beads of different colors for marbles and baby doll hair.

My paternal grandmother's house was just a few doors down the street from Congo Square (now Louis Armstrong Park) in the French Quarter. By the time I was seven years old, my mother and father had moved to the West Bank of the Mississippi River, which meant that we had two bases from which to participate in

Carnival: New Orleans proper *and* the City of Algiers across the river in Jefferson parish.

My extended family got together on holidays such as Christmas and Easter and on special occasions such as weddings and funerals. We had our differences like most families, but we took care of our young and always respected our elders. We were supportive of each other in times of need and could stand strong in defense of the family when necessary. As I recall, Maw-Maw (my father's mother) was a force to contend with in the New Orleans family, and my mother, Irene, was (and still is) the Queen of her household, and indeed our neighborhood. There were two things, however, that tended to divide us a bit: religion and Mardi Gras.

My mother had been raised as a Catholic, and upon his deathbed, her father (Poppa) exacted a promise from her to have all his grandchildren christened Catholic so that we would not become "sanddancers" (which is what I am today, by choice). My father's family belonged to the African Methodist Episcopal Church, and their pride and their hope was in it. My mother and I attended mass while my father played piano and sang in the choir at his church. Two disruptions eventually reconciled this difference: First, my father got in an argument with somebody over something, walked out of his church in anger, and hung up his choir robe. Second, the priest informed my mother that she could not take communion because she had committed the mortal sin of marrying a Protestant man. So the issue of "Which religion?" simply came to an impasse.

Mardi Gras, on the other hand, caused great consternation for many years. It was, and still is, the subject of heated debate. Those who are Catholic at heart feel that Mardi Gras is important because of its relationship to Lent. The Protestants, by contrast, tend to feel that both Mardi Gras and Lent constitute idolatry.

On the issue of participation in the holiday, my mother and my Aunt Marybelle Reed were proud to be handkerchief dancers. They would dress in blue jeans and white blouses and tie red and white bandanas around their heads, and then they would dance down the street waving handkerchiefs and flirting with the crowd in rhythm to the music. My father would try to limit the children's participation to standing on the *banquette* (the sidewalk), where we could catch the goodies thrown from the Carnival floats. He was concerned about the drunkenness and the fighting that inevitably occurred at Mardi Gras. Moma, however, insisted that with proper protection the children could participate in the parades as they passed through the "safe parts of town." Usually this meant that we went to the parade in the town of Algiers and watched the ones in the city of New Orleans on television.

But the real splitting of hairs and gnashing of teeth was reserved for debating the value of the Zulu Parade. (We will examine that more closely later in this chapter.) It seemed that the entire community had one of two opinions: (1) that it was about time colored folks had something of their own, or (2) that it was a shame before God for colored folks to make such fools of themselves just to be in the Mardi Gras. When I was about nine years old my nanan (godmother) took me to the Zulu Parade in New Orleans. There I saw people dressed up like baby dolls, and a devil took a jab at me with his pitchfork. It all seemed very chaotic and more than I could process at the time. I withdrew my mind from the ongoing Zulu debate and made myself content with the candy, jewelry, and toys that other people brought in from Mardi Gras.

Twenty years later I attended a Carnival in New Orleans. A brother, two cousins, and an uncle who knew the ways escorted me. With them at my side I felt secure enough to let the good times roll.

An Introduction to Spring: The Spring Maiden

It begins in Spring. The seeds that have been lying peacefully in the Earth during Winter's dormancy begin to push their way through the casing. Clouds give forth their blessings in the form of rain. The gentle warm rays of the Sun provide quickening, urging the barren trees to turn green with baby blossoms. Their fragrance perfumes the air. We inhale this scent, and the waters of our bodies begin to bubble. Like newborn babies we giggle and preen. We dance within ourselves; our joy is hard to suppress.

We long for *recreation*. Perhaps it begins with a tune, a little finger-popping, head-snapping, hip-shaking tune. We take a plunge in blue water or a bath in the warmth of a bright yellow Sun. Then the Spring waters begin to well up inside of us. We go in search of flowers, for a colorful hat. Imagining that a walk in the park is what we're after, we first stop in a record shop or run through the local florist. It satisfies the urge—temporarily—but the desire to reach out and touch the hand of another is what we're really after. Love is what we are seeking. Love in all its forms: love of Life, love of Earth, love of self, friend, and mate.

Oshun, the Daughter of Promise, intoxicates us with Her honey; we are caught in Her web. She pulls us toward the water, the flowers, the warmth of the Sun. Our bodies want to press close together, then pull away again. We are caught in Her tease. She teases us into a game of Re-Creation. And all of us—plant, animal, and human—respond to the bubbling fertility of Earth, the hunger for birth.

The barren trees turn green with baby blossoms.

The Spring Equinox

The Light from the Sun began to increase with the Winter Solstice. Now, at the Spring Equinox, night and day are of equal length. Hereafter the days will become longer until the Sun reaches its zenith at the Summer Solstice.

Most mythologies have a Goddess who brings on the sunshine. In European mythology the Spring Maiden is seen as the youngest aspect of the Feminine Trinity—Maiden, Mother, and Crone. This trinity has been revered since the advent of agriculture some 12,000 years ago. The Maiden is always a symbol for the renewal of the Earth. Sometimes She is seen as the flow of sweet water (river, rain, waterfall). The rain brought fertility to the plant and animal life of the forest where humans first gathered edible plants and hunted animals for their hides. She is the productivity of the fields.

With the invention of irrigation, the wild lands became controllable farms. River water was brought inland to nurture the Earth, thereby producing food in abundance. Crop surpluses could be used to barter for goods and create wealth, and seeds could be stored for seasonal planting. Through the Maiden, financial security was born, so She is often regarded as the Wealth Giver, or the Abundant One. And just as She stimulated the growth of flowers, the genitalia of the plants, She also came to represent human sexual desire and the impulse to create.

This Goddess has many names in many cultures. In Egypt She is known as Hathor, the Winged Cow of Creation. The Greeks called Her Aphrodite, the "titillator." In India She is the beautiful and prosperous Laksmi. The Anglo-Saxon Goddess is Ostara. She is Indara of Indonesia and the ever-renewing Haumea of the Hawaiian Islands. In the Peruvian Andes She is Cocamama, the

Abundance, joy, and beauty.

matron of the coca plant and women's sexuality. In the Yucatan She is Ix Chel; among the Apache, Painted Woman. In Haiti She is Erzulie, the "irresistible." In African nations She is Oshun Panchagara, Queen of the Fertility Fest.

Some of the tales about the Spring Maiden exalt Her as the

bringer of abundance, joy, and beauty (as symbolized by Hathor). Others say She gave the world things it never should have had (as symbolized by Pandora). Most of the tales depict Her as generous, promiscuous, and beautiful (as symbolized by Oshun).

At Spring Equinox we plant seeds in our gardens, clean the worries of winter from our homes, and celebrate Persephone's ascent from the underworld. In the Western world, the principle of renewal and its various celebrations and original symbols have been obscured by the rituals of the Christian faith that have been handed down to us in the holiday known as Easter.

Easter

The story of Easter is very well known to most of us. It goes something like this:

> When he was twelve years old, Mary's little boy told her that he couldn't keep her company anymore because he had to be about his father's work. She didn't mind. She understood. The boy hung out with Joseph and others and learned many things.
>
> Somewhere between his late twenties and early thirties the young man began to hang out with a group of men now known as the disciples. They sat around drinking wine and talking about the way things ought to be, and they eventually decided to show the people how to behave. So they raided the money houses and performed a host of magical acts, such as

turning water into wine and feeding hungry people. All these activities caused a problem for the people in power, who accused the young man of nefarious doings.

One of his buddies, a fellow named Judas, betrayed him at a banquet known as the Last Supper. Judas pointed the finger at him in exchange for thirty pieces of silver. The government pounced on him, gave him a trial in a kangaroo court, and then executed him along with two other "criminals." Back in those days (before lynching, the electric chair, and lethal injections), the condemned were nailed to a wooden cross (some say it was actually an X), the forefather of the crucifix. They would hang there for days, exposed on a mountaintop, bleeding into the Earth. This public display served as a deterrent to others.

Several women came to see him as he hung from the cross. (In many cultures mourning is the province of women.) They included his mother, Our Mary, and another interesting woman named Mary Magdalene, the Whore of Babylon.

The Marys cried. He died. His body was taken down from the cross. Three days later, when they went to fetch the body for burial, they discovered that "He is risen," and the first Easter Sunday was born.

—Luisah Teish

This is a very touching story that most people can identify with because it features a cultural hero who, supported by the power of the divine, struggles on behalf of the common people, is accused and betrayed, and displays courage in the face of great danger. He was given the power to transcend the adversity, and in so doing leaves a shining example of the best of human possibility and some guidelines for how to achieve excellence. It is a classical hero myth, and similar stories can be found in every culture in the world, including those that predate Christianity.

In Western culture both Catholics and Protestants revere this event with a Sunrise service in their respective churches. Then they come home to a celebration of food and gifts. Usually the gifts are baskets full of fruit, chocolate candy, and brightly colored chicken eggs that are delivered by a bunny rabbit wearing a flowered bonnet. What does this have to do with Mary's son? The symbolism associated with Easter is related to the increase of the Sun's strength and its affect on the Earth's fertility. The Egg is a cosmogenetic symbol representing potency and the possibility of birth everywhere in the world. The yolk of the egg resembles the Sun and fire, and the white of the egg can be seen as the Moon and water. (And the practice of eating raw eggs to increase virility is well known.) We dye the hard-cooked eggs beautiful colors and place them in a basket of straw, which resembles a bird's nest. The reproductive habits of the rabbit and its role in pregnancy testing are also well known. When a pregnancy test comes out positive, some women say "The rabbit died"; a woman who has several children in a short period of time is accused of "reproducing like a rabbit." The rabbit of Easter is the Moonhare. The Easter bonnet, covered with flowers, celebrates the astrological sign Aries, which rules the human head and begins on March 21, the Spring Equinox.

A major calendar event for both Catholics and Protestants, Easter is their "moveable feast," as it always occurs on the first Sunday after the Full Moon *following* the Spring Equinox. Once Easter is established, all other moveable feasts are placed, and the year is set in order. Like many other holidays, Easter is built upon the lunar calendar and shares in the mythology of earlier North African, Middle Eastern, and Indo-European celebrations.

Easter takes its name from the Anglo-Saxon fertility Goddess Ostara, or sometimes Eostre-Oshtara, whose name means "east." She was regarded as a Maiden clothed in the colors of the Sun. She was responsible for the fertility of the fields, especially the new growth that appeared in Spring. Fires were lit at dawn in Her honor, and eggs were dyed bright colors of yellow, orange, and red and offered to Her. She is also associated with the North African Goddesses Astarte and Hathor.

Agricultural societies had a mythological figure known as the Grain King. He was often the Son and/or lover of the Goddess. Sheep-herding societies offered up the wool and blood of a lamb to ensure fertility. Jesus, the Son of Mary, the Maiden Mother, is often called the "Lamb of God." There are many similarities between the stories surrounding Jesus and those of the Grain King. Both figures are born of a Virgin Mother, both are sacrificed for the good of the people, and both are renewed (resurrected) in Spring.

77

Spring

Mardi Gras

Mardi Gras literally means "Fat Tuesday"—the day before Ash Wednesday, which is the day before Lent begins. Traditionally, the common people burn the last of the oil in their lamps, cook red beans and rice with big chunks of salt pork, and say farewell to meat for the Lenten season. *Mardi* means "Tuesday" in French, and the French word *gras* means "fat" and "of good cheer" and implies a time of relaxed morals and merrymaking—presumably in anticipation of the upcoming weeks of Lenten deprivation.

In Rome, a ritual indulgence in sensuality and the fruit of the vine performed in honor of the Greek God of wine (Bacchus) became known as the Bacchanalia. Revelers dressed in animal costumes pelted each other with flowers, drank the fruit of the vine, and paid homage to the Maiden. Today the bacchanalian rite has survived in the seasonal celebration known to us as Carnival, a European holiday that is equivalent to Mardi Gras and is a celebration of Earth's renewal, the fertility of Spring. The word *Carnival* has been translated as *Carne vale,* "Farewell to meat," and *Car navale,* which describes the decorated floats and boats used in European and Egyptian processions. The European holiday of Carnival has been transported to many places in the world such as Rio de Janeiro, New Orleans, and San Francisco.

Carnival in New Orleans started as a French affair. Louisiana's elite society was famous for giving impressive parties, but generally they were private, by invitation only. The earliest recorded Carnival in North America took place in New Orleans in 1704.

Between 1718 and 1799 these parties became more public. As a means of controlling criminals, the Spanish outlawed masquerading, but the French, a party-loving people, continued to promote it, and by 1824 Carnival was very popular and the masquerading was legalized. But Mardi Gras did not become "tradition" in the United States until 1827, when it was promoted by a group of students returning from Paris, where they had celebrated it annually.

Secret Societies

Carnival organizations are secret societies commonly called "krewes." Each krewe has a theme for the parade, which requires long-range planning, specialized costumes, songs, dances, floats, and pageant dramas. Most krewes begin their "work" (which includes fundraising, parties, and fashion shows) just after Christmas, and it goes on almost every night until Mardi Gras in February. Louisiana Carnivals have traditionally based their characters on local Earth-centered themes. The first Carnival floats (1837) related to agriculture. The King and Queen were named *de la Feve,* after a large edible bean, and their props were farming tools. Little boys representing the Son of the Goddess pelted people below the float with sacks of flowers as it passed by. The Mardi Gras krewes were often dedicated to aspects of the Grain King. In 1857 the Mystick Krewe of Father Comus, the Roman God of joy, was formed. And Rex, the first "King" of Carnival, appeared in 1872. By 1875 Mardi Gras had become a legal holiday. Today the Rex Parade is the pinnacle of this Spring rite.

On the surface, Mardi Gras appeared to be simply a time to get drunk and act out. But beneath its powdered face it was a politico-spiritual movement that celebrated ancient folk beliefs and subtly influenced the government of the city. The King of Mardi Gras has the power to reverse the social order for a period of time, much like the King of Fools did in the Roman Saturnalia.

Most of this celebrating occurred against a backdrop of Black slavery. The Emancipation Proclamation was not issued until 1863, so Black people participated in Carnival behind the scenes as servants, spectators in the crowd, and torchbearers alongside the parade. It was not until 1910 that Black people formed their own krewe and gave birth to the controversial Zulu Parade.

The Zulu Parade

As a child I could not understand the debate over the Zulu Parade. Now I recognize that the Zulu Parade bespeaks remnants of old African customs. It contains elements of ancestor reverence that have been maintained in the culture underground, in spite of slavery, poverty, and racism. The Zulu paint their faces with white chalk, just like the devotees of Olokun and Mami Wata presented in chapter 1. Because of racist conditioning, pollywogs and the minstrel shows immediately come to mind, but marking the face with white chalk is a precolonial spiritual tradition in many parts of Africa, especially in West Africa, the Motherland of most Black Americans. The chalk (koalin, efun, or cascarilla) is usually taken from the sediment of the river or the belly of caves. Each source is regarded as an important body part of Mother Earth, and white chalk on Black faces puts one, chromatically, between the physical and the spiritual worlds, between the living and the dead. The Zulus of Mardi Gras wear raffia skirts made from the fiber of the palm leaf. In many African traditions raffia is used to adorn the ceremonial hut, to dress the altars of deities, and to cover the bodies of masqueraders in African ancestral festivals.

> William Story was the first king [of the Zulu Parade], wearing a lard-can crown and carrying a banana-stalk scepter. By 1913 progress had reached the point where King Peter Williams wore a starched white suit and an onion stickpin and carried a loaf of Italian bread as a scepter. In 1914 King Henry rode in a buggy, and from that year they grew increasingly ambitious, boasting three floats in 1940, entitled, respectively, "The Pink Elephant," on which rode the King and his consort, "Hunting the Pink Elephant," and "Capturing the Pink Elephant."[3]

The banana stalk, the onion stickpin, and the bread all represent the fertility of the Goddess because they grow in the body of the Earth. King Henry, like the great Hannibal, chose the elephant to signify royalty. The elephant is sacred to Obatala, the Cloud King presented in chapter 1. In Africa, it is the elephant, not the lion, who is regarded as king of the jungle. And the threatened extinction of this ancient beast is an omen to us all.

In 1922 the reigning Zulu King reenacted another important African tradition. He rented a yacht—the Royal Barge—and rode

81

it in high style down the New Basin Canal. In Africa (which includes Egypt), political dignitaries parade downriver to survey their realm and to visit neighboring royalty. Initiations into sacred priesthoods in Africa often begin with a ritual at the river. And in Nigeria the great Feminine Force is Oshun, the Goddess of the River. So again we have symbolic intercourse between the Grain King and the Spring Maiden.

The Zulu Kings wore majestic costumes, held court, and dispensed coconuts to the revelers. When a Zulu King died, his body was escorted by a grand marshal, sixteen pallbearers, and a thirteen-piece brass band that played "I'll Be Glad When You're Dead, You Rascal You."

The Black Indians

In addition to Zulu kings and queens, baby dolls, and devils, the Black people of New Orleans also paid homage to the ancestors of the land. They created the Krewe of the Black Indians (circa 1920). The early participants were of African American and Native American descent. (It is estimated that one out of every five Black people in this country has some Native American ancestry.)

But participation in the Black Indian parade was not based on ancestry alone. It was also based on affinity with the culture and a history of cooperative living between some Africans and Native Americans. This is a history that has been kept out of the schoolbooks. The Black Indians in the Carnival of New Orleans took Native American names, made splendid costumes, created songs in traditional Native rhythms, and endured the ordeal of becoming chief.

> The Golden Blades were started twenty-five years ago in a saloon. Ben Clark was the first chief and ruled until two years ago, when a younger man took over. Leon Robinson—Chief Happy Peanut—deposed Clark in actual combat, as is the custom.... That's the way a chief is created, and that is the way his position is lost.[4]

Again we see a subtext of food (Happy Peanut) and of humor and the harvest (golden blades). Still we have a hint of a chief, king, or son who is connected to the land, who shines for a period of time, and then is cut down and dies.

St. Joseph's Day

The Catholic season of Lent begins on Ash Wednesday, forty days (Sundays not included) before Easter. On Ash Wednesday, a priest (sometimes a visiting bishop) places ashes on devotees' foreheads and says, "Remember, man, that thou art dust, and to dust thou shalt return." (In recent years priests have had the option of using a different, self-composed statement of faith.) The ash is the mark of death and sorrow. On Ash Wednesday and Good Friday, Catholics observe a partial fast (only one meal a day), and during the entire Lenten season they sacrifice one of their favorite foods (meat, eggs, sweets), impose a behavioral taboo on themselves (no booze, no sex, no something), or take some positive action (volunteer at a homeless shelter, participate in the various religious services offered only during Lent) as a reminder of their observance. It is a time to release, to forgive, to meditate. The Lenten fast precedes the Easter feast. In New Orleans, a mid-Lent respite from austerity was found in the celebration of St. Joseph's Day, also known as Joe Worker's Day.

Saint Joseph, the husband of Mary, was a humble and hard-working man. He was a carpenter of Nazareth, a descendant of David of Bethlehem, and a widower. Little is said about him in the first two chapters of the manuscripts of Matthew and Luke, and other characters, such as John the Baptist (whom we will discuss in the next chapter) often overshadow him. Even today, Saint Joseph is considered a great example of a kind husband and good father, and he is believed to have rulership over employment and marriage. In New Orleans, common people—especially Italians and Catholic African Americans—emulate his life. His official feast day is May 1, but in New Orleans he is celebrated on March 19.

His holiday is one of conspicuous display and sharing. Celebrants set a large statue of Saint Joseph on the dining table and place before him several kinds of bread, an abundance of seafood, and various desserts. Poor neighbors and orphans are invited to eat, and money offerings and prayers are left at the foot of the saint in hopes that "Saint Joe the Worker" will get to work on the petitioner's problem. The people's relationship to Saint Joe is friendly and intimate. People pray and talk to him; they cry and laugh with him. Bread, lucky beans (fava beans), and bay leaf are given out.

Some people display their Carnival costumes on this occasion. But at the stroke of midnight all the feasting stops, and the austerity of Lent resumes.

And if, after three days, Saint Joe has not granted the petition, his image is taken out of the house and stood on its head until he starts "working."

We did not set the table for Saint Joe in my neighborhood. But we regarded him as an example of a good man, and people looking for employment or seeking good marriages carried a card of him in their pockets. I must say that on more than one occasion Joe has worked for me.

A Celebration of Persephone

Spring Equinox, Negril, Jamaica, circa 1991. We stood atop a mountain composed of white coral and green trees. An opening in the Earth between the rocks invited me to investigate its mystery. Moving slowly, cautiously, I slid down the rocks an inch at a time until I was just beneath the surface of the mountain.

Now the roots of the great trees above me hang, long and strong. They extend all the way down to the floor of this cave. I steady myself by holding onto two great roots, like a child in a swing. I use them to move from stone to stone, going deeper into the Earth. This is a cave, but ironically not a dark one, because sunlight shines in from above through another portal in the Earth.

One by one the members of my party (five women and three

men) climb down the rocks, gaping in wonder at the sight of the sunlight in the belly of the Earth. And even more profound than the light is the great silence here in the world of Persephone, who, according to pre-Christian Western mythologies, lived half her life—during the sleep of Winter—under the Earth in Hades, and the other half—during the blossoming of Spring—above the surface of the Earth. We stand transfixed by the silence, then slowly begin to move into the space. There are two distinct features here: large vulva-shaped figures in stone—natural formations that seem to emerge from the cave floor—and one wall of the cave with many holes in it. With a little imagination I can see an apartment complex with sculptures in a rock garden. And that's exactly what the wall was—a hotel for hermit crabs.

As we moved deeper into the cave, the hermit crabs (at least twenty of them) came out of their holes to observe the intruders. The sound of their claws and shells tapping on the stone was both sacred and scary. We froze and remained still. Soon the crabs found us boring and returned to their homes, perhaps to take an afternoon nap.

But the humans were fascinated with what we'd seen and where we were. At first we sat in silent meditation, and then a truly magical thing happened. Someone, I don't remember who, made a guttural sound. Others began to hum, and others started to walk around the space, touching the sculptures. Soon we were chanting:

Ancient Mother, we hear you calling.
Ancient Mother, we feel your tears.

Ancient Mother, oh please forgive us.
Ancient Mother, remove our fears.

This is a variation of a popular pagan chant. We found ourselves hugging the stones and crying. We made a small fire and sat around it in silence, as sunlight streamed into the cave. I have no idea how long we sat there in the silence, but soon a gentle rain began to fall on the land above. We stood there with our eyes closed, kissed by raindrops, facing the sun. Then, like Persephone, we ascended from the depths to the surface of the Earth, into a field of wildflowers.

I love Jamaica in the Spring.

A Celebration of Oshun

The shrine of the Goddess Oshun is located in Oshogbo, Nigeria, where Her river flourishes. The Royal Palace of the Ataoja (the king of Oshogbo) sits in a sacred grove, lush with palm trees and other tropical plants. The courtyard floor is an ancient mosaic of cowry shells and kola nuts. The roots of the great trees go underground and then curve up as if they were serpents traversing the middle ground between the underworld and the surface of the Earth. The tops of those trees embrace each other, in places, and streams of sunlight penetrate the green cathedral. Here, Heaven, Earth, and the Underworld meet, and the River Oshun nourishes them all. The musical voices of Her priestesses echo through the grove:

Oore ye ye O–Beautiful Mother O

Oore ye ye O-Beautiful Mother O
Oshun O pe O-River I am calling you
Oshun Ro, ye ye O-Beautiful Mother appear.

The Power, Humor, and Wisdom of Oshun

Oshun is the Maiden-Mother-Queen. Like Mawu, She is the moisture that balances the blazing heat of the Sun. Her shrine in Oshogbo, Nigeria, is the coolest place in town.

Yoruba mythology attributes many powers to Her, and there are many myths in which She has the leading role. Oshun need only withdraw Her powers and creation shrivels and dies. She is the Powerful Maiden.

One story says that the art of divining was the exclusive property of Obatala, the King of the White Cloth, and Orunmila, the Diviner of Destiny. Oshun learned the system at Her own expense and then taught it to everyone else for free. She is the Generous Queen.

The Orature says that in Her vulture aspect (Ibukole), She carries our prayers and offerings to Heaven on Her mighty wings. So great was this task that She gave birth to Elegba, the Messenger, so that He could share the work. She is the Wise Mother.

Oshun is sophisticated, a leader among women. She inspires us in the arts, business, and public relations. She is the Gracious Lady.

Late at night, when the Bird Women known as "the Mothers" gather in the tops of the Sacred Palm Tree, it is Oshun who leads the flock. They share the secrets only women know: how to fly

ठठ
Jump Up

backward and upside down, how to turn blood into babies. She is the Woman of Mystery.

Tradition says that She is married to Orunmila, but She has attraction to and intimate relationships with several other Orishas, especially Shango, the Lord of Thunder, Lightning, and Fire, and Ogun, the Wildman in the Woods. When Ogun is raging in the forest, the trees tremble and the animals stampede to escape His wrath. Oshun dresses Herself in five yellow silk scarves and scents Herself with amber. Then She smears honey on the raging man's lips. It soothes and tames the wildness. Her sweet water moistens the roots of the trees, and sap pulses through their trunks, limbs, and branches.

In a storm of jealousy Shango sends His lightning bolts to set the trees ablaze. The forest fire rages, consuming herbs and flowers, tumbling great trees, scorching the Earth. The Lady watches in admiration, smiling at His display of passion. When His heat has fertilized the seeds lying dormant under the Earth, She dances in His direction, undulating to the rhythm of His thunder. As Spring rain falls, She quenches His thirst.

In most of the stories, Oshun uses Her gift of attraction to change the balance of power between the deities, to bring fertility to the land, and to inspire joy in the hearts of humans. When the indigenous African traditions came to the Americas they merged with Catholicism, and Oshun became identified with Mary. But Mary's femininity is neutered. She doesn't menstruate, she doesn't mate, and she doesn't nurse her child. This is not so with Oshun.

89

Spring

As a consequence of Western eros-phobia and the Madonna-whore complex, Oshun's image has suffered. Today in Cuba She is referred to as *La Puta Santa* (the Whore Saint) and is envisioned as a prostitute of interracial ancestry. This is not the African image. This image speaks to the political and cultural history of the Western Hemisphere. By identifying Her with Mary, "New World" devotees misunderstood the power of Her intercourse and reduced Her to a simple coquette.

She is my personal Goddess. I have a respectful and intimate relationship with Her. The story that follows is just one expression of Her power, Her humor, and Her crazy wisdom.

The Hilarious Lady

In typical Teish fashion I stood before my shrine, legs apart, arms extended skyward with a bell in one hand and a palm leaf fan in the other. I'd placed before Oshun the offerings of honey, gold cloth, fragrant flowers, and money (Susan B. Anthony dollars), artistically arranged on a palm frond mat. I was dressed in yellow silk with bells on my ankles and a bright red parrot feather in my green and yellow gele (head wrap). Gentle sunlight streamed through the door of my shrine room, and a shower of delicate pink and white plum blossoms drifted past the window. It was Spring (circa 1991), and I had paradise in my own backyard.

I rang the Goddess's bell and asked Her to "send me Abundance, today." I followed my request with a song, which grew into a dance and then ended in senseless laughter. I put down my sacred objects, lit my yellow candle, and sprayed the room with perfume (Her personal brand). As I gave the offering a last critical examination, my doorbell upstairs rang. I sprinted up the stairs. There in the doorway stood a friend of mine, a son of Shango. His eyes sparkled, and he flashed a mischievous smile. Huh? I wondered what the man was up to. He announced that he had brought me "a gift" and had placed it in the backyard. We walked past the plum trees, the morning glory vines, and the mustard greens, and then I found his "gift." There on a bed of freshly turned Earth sat a box full of baby bunny rabbits. Yes! Baby bunny rabbits. Eleven of them—five black, five white, and one black and white. They were beautiful—but they were bunnies! What was I to do?

It didn't take long for the neighborhood kids to hear about my great gift. And in a day or two I had managed to yield to the pleading eyes of the children. I gave the bunnies away, packed a suitcase (to escape the wrath of the mothers), and landed in Hilo, Hawaii, for a Spring Equinox celebration.

About 200 participants (led by my friend and sister Starhawk) gathered in a lush green field under a moonlit sky. One of the young people, about five years old and dressed in leaves and flowers, stood beside me. I turned to an adult and said, "I see that the fairies are out tonight." There was a slight tug on my *malo* (Hawaiian wraparound skirt), and a small voice whispered "I'm not a fairy. . . . I'm a little girl." I touched my lips with my fingers and agreed to keep our secret.

Soon it was my turn to tell a story. I talked about the Goddess'

sense of humor. Then I recounted the ritual I'd performed before my altar asking the Goddess for abundance, the day the rabbits appeared. From out of the darkness, far across the field, a voice called out, "She thought you said, 'A Bunny Dance.'" And the whole field laid down in laughter. Unexpected joy is the name of Oshun.

Spring, the Daughter of Promise

Children will not be wanting at the hand of
the mother; young children will not be wanting
at the foot of the banana tree.
—The Holy Odu Ogbe Meji

There in the garden stood a creature made from the desire of Moon, composed in the likeness of Sun. There in the garden stood a creature made from the desire of Sun, made in the image of Moon. They stood looking at each other, uncertain of who they were and how they came into Being.

Sensing their dilemma, the Serpent opened its mouth and spat forth a rain of knowledge followed by a shower of love. The two creatures gazed at each other, their hearts pounding in their chests. Slowly the Sun and Moon within them began to stir until they could only embrace and mingle their substances in a dance of delight.

As they danced, the banana tree rumbled and produced long yellow fruit. As they danced, the Earth shook and produced millet. They danced and all existence multiplied itself. The Divine Twins felt the fertility of the Earth pulse through them and spread from them to the land and back again. And they laughed because it was Spring.

—Luisah Teish, original tale, 1988

Using the Sacred Palm in Rituals

The palm tree is sacred to the Goddess Oshun, and it is important to many other deities as well. Orunmila, the Diviner of Destiny, uses palm nuts as an oracle. The Warriors (Elegba, Ogun, and a hunter named Ochossi) receive palm oil as part of their offering. The grass skirts worn by the Goddess Oya and by Omolu (the deity of infectious diseases) are made of palm leaves. And the mats that devotees pray and eat on are made of palm fronds. The African Vulture, the bird of Oshun Ibukole, eats palm nuts as a part of her regular diet.

In North Africa the palm tree is sacred to the Goddess Isis. It is regarded as a symbol of victory, fame, and exaltation. In some parts of Egypt Moslems paint the fronts of their houses in bright colors and plant a palm tree near the front door to indicate that they have made the Hadji, the pilgrimage to Mecca, their Holy city. In the Christian tradition, Palm Sunday is the Sunday before Easter, and it celebrates Jesus' entry into Jerusalem. The folklore says that the people laid palm branches in his path. The practice of laying leaves and flowers before a revered person is widespread and ancient.

93

Spring

There are a number of rituals that are performed with the palm tree:

- In France the graves of relatives are decorated with blessed palm leaves.
- In Puerto Rico palm leaves are woven into crosses, which are hung in the house for protection and abundance.
- In Belgium pieces of blessed palm are placed in the fields to assure a good harvest.
- In Cuba family members sweep each other with blessed palm branches to ward off evil spirits.
- In New Orleans palmetto palms are planted near a pond on one's property to assure health, luck, and love.

Think about it. How many ways do you use palm products?

Suggestions for Celebrating Spring

I've always loved the awakening of Spring. For me it usually begins with the shower of plum blossoms in my backyard. Then the birds begin to place their nests on the branches, and the other critters who live in my backyard start to flourish. The simple act of going to the grocery store is made more pleasant by the crop of babies in their strollers, out now for a view of the new world. It is a wonderful time to linger in the sweet sunlight. Here are a few recommendations for enhancing your Spring experience.

The Great Egg Give-Away

Most of us grew up with the practice of hunting for Easter eggs. This was fun until I realized that my brother was cheating. Here's an idea that can bring your children into a relationship with the season that is both sacred and fun.

Many variety stores sell bags of multicolored plastic eggs that are designed to be taken apart and filled with candy. These bags usually have at least a dozen plastic eggs and only cost about $2. Your local nursery probably sells large buckets of indigenous wildflower seeds. These usually cost about $5. Add to the plastic eggs and the wildflower seeds a basket with straw, and you are ready to begin.

Lay several paper towels on the table, then place a large bowl, a cooking spoon, and the basket next to them. Place the wildflower seeds in the bowl and invite the children to stir the seeds with their hands while naming their "good wishes" for the family. For example, "I wish that Uncle Joe would get well; I wish that all the sad people could be happy...." Let them determine the wishes. Encourage them to create a chant or poem. Then, using the cooking spoon, put one spoonful of wildflower seeds in each egg, close it, and put it in the basket. The children can have the pleasure of giving these eggs to relatives and friends as a blessing from future generations. If the relative or friend is a gardener, the child will also have the pleasure of seeing their gift grow into beautiful flowers.

Persephone's Wildflower Field

When I was young and ambitious (those pre–back injury days), I used to garden from March 20 to 24. I mean I used to garden nonstop. During those four days I would not leave my backyard. I'd till, plant, water, and dream. I didn't do anything else, especially not answer the phone. My message machine had a long-playing tape in it that could be replaced with another. So my household would simply stack them up for my listening when my planting frenzy was over.

This particular year (circa 1987), I began my March 25 tape-listening marathon and heard a series of messages with an interesting progression. The first day's tape carried an offer to go to Peru, all-expenses paid, for the Harmonic Convergence. The second day's tape was a repeat of the first message and a request to call back as soon as I got the message. The third day's tape explained that if I didn't call back that day, they would have to give my ticket to someone else. The fourth day's tape said how sorry they were that I hadn't responded. Now on the fifth day, I was listening to an offer to go to Iowa. All I could say was, "I guess the Goddess wants me to see America first."

I don't want you to get as absorbed as I was back then, but I must say that my garden was exquisite. Garden on your own time and in your own way. There is a lot of material on low-maintenance gardening and many Earth-friendly products you can use. I recommend that you go to your local nursery and ask for a tub of butterfly or hummingbird scatter. Prepare your yard, then scatter

these seeds according to the directions on the box, and watch your
yard turn into paradise.

The Seasonal Table or Altar

Spring cleaning and decorating the house are beautiful processes,
especially if you turn on the music while you work. Many people
are pleased to place a wreath of Spring flowers on their porch or
front door, and others brighten the room with tulips and daffodils.

　　You may want to create a seasonal altar for Spring. Simply cover
a small table with a piece of cloth, perhaps one with a floral pattern
or a sensuous silky one. Place a bowl of water in the center with an
object representing your favorite Spring symbol (a statue of Quan
Yin, a large agate egg, or an extra tall Spring green candle). Float
the petals of your favorite flower, preferably something fragrant like
rose petals or freesia, in the water. My personal favorite is night-
blooming jasmine. Now you can place your meal around this centerpiece or use it as the altar for your seasonal rituals.

Praise Singing the Earth

Earth Day occurs in the month of April, usually on or around the
22nd of the month. On this day many organizations concerned
with the environment hold meetings and celebrations to increase
awareness of local issues and to recruit the energies of the community to deal with those issues. It is important to know the soil you
are growing in, and Earth Day is a wonderful day to connect with
the Spirit of the Earth through a simple praise singing.

Begin by standing—either by yourself or together with friends and family—in your garden or the local park. If a group, stand in a circle and hold hands. Take several slow deep breaths. Feel the sunlight and the wind on your face. Feel the Earth beneath your feet. Tell the Goddess that you marvel at the talent, powers, and beauty contained in every seed, in Spring, in the cells of your body. Allow your power of vision to grow freely. Think of things you would like to be able to do well or better. Now simply speak words of thanks. Thank the Earth for all She has given us. Thank Her for the beauty of Her precious stones, Her delicious water, and Her wonderful flowers. Thank Her for sustaining plant, animal, and human life.

Apologize on behalf of those who have raped and poisoned Her. Then renew your commitment to Her healing and that of Her children. Conjure up creative things that would be great fun to do that are also good for the Earth. See yourself secure in the knowledge that Her power is within you.

Sing songs, eat well, and laugh.

A Spring Ritual

This ritual can be done at any Full Moon during the Spring.

It was performed at the University of Creation Spirituality, Naropa University, Oakland Campus, in Spring 2000. It was open to the community, and many people turned out for this event. I recount it here because it is suitable for a family or community, it is easy to conduct, and it was very beneficial for those who participated. A sample invocation to the directions is given. Please feel free to alter it to suit the needs of your ritual.

Preparation

Dress a table with cloth and place a bowl of bay laurel leaves on it. Place this table near the entry to the ritual.

Provide a place for food on another table. (I recommend a potluck for this event.)

For the center altar, cover a table with cloth. Place flowers, Quan Yin, and other Goddesses in the center. Prepare the directions by placing candles, stones, and bowls as follows:

North: White candle, crystal stone, candied ginger pieces in a bowl

South: Red candle, jasper stone, cinnamon candies in a bowl

East: Yellow candle, amethyst stone, edible sunflower seeds in a bowl

West: Blue candle, black stone, lychee gels (or other sweet) in a bowl

Place two large bowls of water on the altar and place musical instruments on the floor around the altar. Also place a basket to *receive* the laurel leaves.

On another table, put flyers, books, and other items addressing the community's concerns.

Invocation to the Directions

East: Family members should all face the East. A selected person will lead the invocation by verbally creating visions of the power of Seed. Here we describe the potential of seed lying quietly in the dark womb of the Earth. Seed contains the ancestral memory of its genus and species. Describe various seeds: small ones, encased ones, bulbs, and eyes. Feel the seed receiving water, being caressed by the nurturing soil. See the seed bursting open. Blessed be the power of the Seed.

South: Family members should all face the South. A selected person invokes the power of Stalk. Here we see the stalk bursting forth from the seed, pushing its way through the soil, struggling, and breaking ground to feel the clear rays of the first sunlight. As the stalk stretches skyward it also sends its roots deeper into the Earth. The stalk develops strength. Blessed be the power of the Stalk.

West: Family members should all face the West. A selected person invokes the power of Flower. Here we see the flower's bud at the end of the stalk. Flower begins to open, unfolding, displaying itself. Flower is sensuous, and vain. Flower drips nectar, flashes bright colors, fills the air with scent. Flower is beautiful. Blessed be the power of the Flower.

North: Family members should all face the North. A selected person invokes the power of Fruit. Now we see fruit in the great variety of things that Earth gives us to eat. We see squash and corn, lettuce and tomatoes, bananas and oranges. Fruit is the reward of labor and a medicine to those who consume it. Fruit is tasty and abundant. And most important, fruit contains the seed of future possibility. Fruit is fulfillment. Blessed be the power of the Fruit. Return to the center.

Performing the Ritual

Entering: Participants enter, take a laurel leaf at the door, and choose a seat.

Drumming: Begin playing a gentle rhythm. Pass out small instruments. Encourage humming and chanting, which leads to opening song (of your choice). Everyone takes nine slow, deep breaths.

Invoking the Directions: Holding the appropriate stone and lighting the candle, speak to the Ancestors of each direction. Ask for protection of the boundaries; ask for light on the path.

Invoking the Moon: A chosen person or a chorus reads their favorite poem to the Moon.

Invoking the Cycle of Release: The family recites this or some other appropriate invocation:

> Oh Mother Moon, queen of the Hidden Secrets, Wise, Compassionate Light. I, your daughter (name yourself) (or your son), come before you tonight. I come seeking protection, forgiveness, and release. I'm asking for healing, for blessing, for peace.

Anointing: The bowls of water are passed; each person dips his

101

Spring

or her laurel leaf in the water and touches the third eye, the heart, and the navel, followed by nine slow, deep breaths.

Calling the Goddesses: Now call out the names of the Goddesses. The participants chant each name until it crescendos and decrescendos.

Rededicating: Ask the family the question, "How do you know it is Spring?" Speak to being receptive to new life, and ask that they rededicate themselves to growth as they place the laurel leaf on the altar and taste life from the bowls in the directions.

Harmonizing: Beginning with drums, hum together. Then, adding the small instruments, create a harmony that escalates into joyous dancing.

Closing the Ritual: Take nine slow, deep breaths, thank the Goddesses, the ancestors, the directions, and each other. Make announcements, offer food, and so on.

A Spring Recipe: Sunshine Salad

Spring is a time of sweetness and light. In Spring we clean our houses of the dust in the closets, we clean our minds of worries and depression, and some people take a Spring tonic to clean out their bodies. There are many fine products on the market to assist in these cleansings. I use lemon-scented soaps and vanilla-scented powders for my home. But when it comes to body and soul, food is my best medicine. So I offer to you my favorite Sunshine Salad.

Let me say, briefly, that there is a lot of symbolism in this salad. Obviously the pineapple rings and the papaya and orange slices call to mind the relationship between Mawu and Lisa, the Sun and the Moon. Milk and honey have biblical fame, and, of course, you recognize Persephone's famous pomegranate. Pomegranate comes from the French *pomme grenate,* which means "apple with many seeds." It is thought to represent the Yoni and is used in many love spells (though I would be careful of Hades).

Oranges and tangerines are sacred to the Goddess Oshun. They represent Her generosity and Her beauty. Orange blossom water is one of Her favorite perfumes. Pineapple is sacred to Yemaya, the Mother Goddess introduced in chapter 1. It is a sign of hospitality and can be found on the doorways and bedposts of furniture in many Southern homes. Because it has many eyes and wears a leafy crown, it is also associated with protection and with royalty. The coconut, like the palm tree, is held in high regard in the symbolism of the African diaspora. The coconut gives us food (its flesh), water (its milk), medicine (its inner skin), utensils (its outer shell), and guidance (as a divining tool). It is sacred to Obatala, the King of the White Cloth. Bananas are regarded as the phallic fruit of Shango, the deity of Fire, Thunder, and Lightning. It is associated with male virility and business acumen. Its flower is strong and beautiful. Papaya contains the digestive enzyme papain, which assists in absorbing the nutrients of all the other ingredients. The ginger allows us to taste the warmth of the Sun as it tickles our palates and clears our sinuses.

Ingredients

Lettuce leaves, your choice (butter lettuce or banana flowers if you can get them)

1 medium-sized banana

2 medium-sized oranges or tangerine sections, parted and deveined

3 slices of pineapple (I prefer fresh, but canned slices are pretty; watch out for sugar content)

1 medium-sized papaya, seeded and cut in crescent moon slices

¼ cup (a handful) of candied ginger cubes

¼ cup toasted coconut flakes

1 cup of unflavored yogurt (or piña colada-flavored yogurt, if you like it)

2 tablespoons of milk (whole or reduced fat)

Pomegranate (I'm not about to tell you how many pomegranate seeds to eat)

Directions

Line your salad bowl with lettuce leaves.

Place the pineapple rings in the center of the leaves.

Lay the papaya crescents in a circle around the pineapple rings.

Distribute the orange/tangerine pieces with their crescent facing the pineapple rings.

Cut bananas into small cubes and place them in the center of the pineapple rings.

Now mix the yogurt, milk, and honey together in a small bowl. Pour this over the salad.

Distribute the ginger cubes in the body of the salad.

Sprinkle with pomegranate seeds.

Summer

A Personal Encounter with Summer: An Initiation with the Goddess Pele

Summer 1999. It took years, but She finally grew impatient with me and decided to make Her importance clear. I had walked in the shadow of the Goddess Pele for many years before I had the wisdom or perhaps the courage to look directly into the flame. But here I was now, standing on Her sacred ground, properly dressed, with my Ti leaf offering in hand.

I graduated from high school in 1966 and enrolled in a small college in Oregon. The student body there was 10 percent Hawaiian, so I attended luaus, ate chicken long rice, and shared fur coats with brown-skinned women, who, like me, could not endure the snow.

Occasionally, someone would bring me puka shells or macadamia nut candies back from a trip to their tropical island. But I never thought I'd go there.

In the Summer of 1982 I was initiated into the Orisha tradition as a priestess of the Goddess Oshun, whom we discussed at length in chapters 1 and 2. That initiation, like those of ancient Egypt, began with a mandatory bath in the river. Because I couldn't get to the

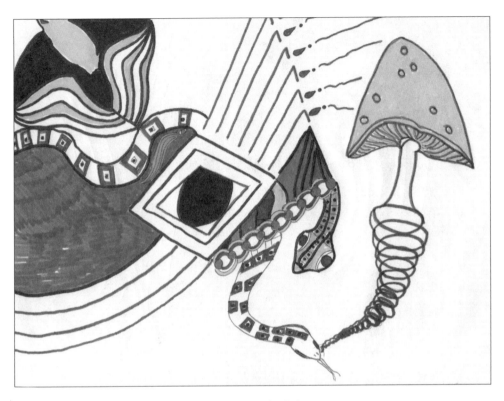

Spirit moves both in and out, between and through all things.

Nile I had to settle for the local mountain stream. It was almost midnight before the elders, who were flying in from all over the Western Hemisphere, arrived. And although I would have preferred a bath under a blazing sun, my bath took place in the middle of the night, somewhere in the hills of Oakland, California. Three women elders wrapped me in white cloth and placed me in the car. My husband David was driving that night. Somewhere between the house and the river our car broke down. I don't remember now whether it was a flat tire or if the battery had gone dead. Whatever the problem was, David decided to park the car off the road, in the bush, for safety's sake, while he went for help. I sat there in mandatory silence while the elders made comments that were designed to make me afraid of the initiation process. It was all very funny . . . to them.

And then the tables turned. We heard a strange noise in the bush. One elder was from out of town, the other was from a different state, and the third was from another country. They didn't know the Bay Area and began to worry about bears, Big Foot, and zombies. I sat in mandatory silence. The bushes rumbled, and David (a son of Ogun, the Wildman in the Woods) emerged from the dark accompanied by a man and a woman, both Hawaiian, both medicine people who understood what we were up to. They helped us fix the car, went to the spot with us, and waited a respectful distance until we were finished. Then they said "Aloha" after they knew we were safely on our way. But still I didn't get it.

On the fourth day of my initiation (it's a seven-day process) the elders "fed the Sun" to acquire "Sacred time." During this time, extensive divination was performed to ascertain the myths and rituals that would guide me through the rest of my life. On the very first casting of the shells, there was silence and then a great noise! The elders spoke in several languages among themselves and rocked and shuffled in their seats, and then Baba (the man who was my primary sponsor) got a brow-knitting headache. Apparently Elegba, the Linguist of the deities, had said something about me and volcano eruptions. But I still didn't realize what was happening, and no one would explain.

It was not until a year and seven days later that I understood what was going on. The initiation process required me to stay in a state of incubation during that entire period of more than a year. I was "untouchable," quiet, and dressed in spotless white clothing every day. The last day of this incubation found me on the island of Maui (the Hawaiian Trickster-Magician). I rose that morning and put on as many colors as I could find: a peacock blue gauze dress, an eggshell-colored slip, a forest green cotton shawl, and a tangerine-colored gele with a bright red parrot feather stuck in it. I walked out into the morning light and encountered one of Maui's exquisite rainbows. I lifted my face and opened my arms to take in the energy and to give thanks for my newfound freedom. At that moment one of the local medicine people came to tell me that on the main island, Pele's volcano had just blown.

That was the Summer of 1983, and She has been blowing steadily ever since.

O Pele O. Great Feminine Fire, Tempestuous Queen. I have learned that I must come to You to cleanse my heart, to renew my Spirit, to temper my fire, to find the courage to keep on keeping on. O Pele O. Respected Lady of the Flame, Sun-Fire nestled in the belly of the Earth. Now I understand that we are sisters across the Sea.

An Introduction to Summer: The Holiest Season

In Summer the Sun shines brightly in the sky. Pack up the office, put the schoolbooks away. Open the windows, pull down the shades, and find your rose-colored glasses. Tuck that tummy into a bathing suit or let it hang out in a billowy frock, puff up your "greedy brim" hat. Repaint the patio furniture, stretch out on the lawn, or pack up a picnic basket and head for the beach.

The children jump up and down for snow cones and ice cream. The adults drink lemonade and iced tea. A parade passes by and everyone waves. Dad takes command of the barbecue pit, Grandma sleeps, and Baby rolls in the sand. Everyone is oiled and dusted or shaded by cloth, to protect them from the Sun's heat.

On warm Summer nights we make fires, sit around them, tell stories, and kiss or laugh in the firelight. The dark sky above us is sprinkled with stars that harbor heroes and gods. This is the time to jump up, celebrate life, and enjoy ourselves with family, neighbors, and friends. Every day of Summer is a holy day, and we are all worshipers of the Sun. Holidays may be "holy days" associated with religious mythology, or they may be days that are "holy" because we regard them as special for social, political, and personal reasons. Most people celebrate the legal and political holidays of their nation, state, and city, such as the Fourth of July or International Women's Day. Various groups have their social holidays when people get together to reinforce their commitment to each other or their appreciation of each other, such as anniversaries or Secretaries Day. And a personal holiday may be preordained, such as a birthday, or created because it is needed, such as a "mental health" day. What makes these days "holy" is our behavior on them and our attitude toward them.

Holidays are characterized by fasts and feasts, by generosity and thanksgiving, and by relaxation and celebration. In my opinion, this makes the entire Summer a season for personal and social holidays.

The Summer Solstice

The Summer Solstice, June 21, is the longest day of the year. Now the Sun has reached its zenith and blazes, in some places mercilessly, down on the Earth. She responds to the Sun's attention with flowers in full bloom and teeming wildlife. The human impulses of Spring are intensified, and we flock to amusement parks, hurl ourselves into the Oceans, and make love in the fields under the warmth of a setting Sun.

In West African folklore, the Sun is acknowledged as a great power but remains aloof from the intimate affairs of human beings. We find a Sun Father who retreats from close contact with life on Earth. Sometimes the Sun just gets tired and decides that He will roll around minding His own business. But more often He is annoyed by human beings (as they ate His clouds for dinner). The heavenly bodies, which are relied upon to shine daily, are recognized in prayer and may on occasion even receive offerings. And, although the Sun is important to all life on Earth, in tropical climates the rain, rather than the Sun, is the Great Gift, and Thunder and Lightning may command more attention from the people. This annoys the Sun. And sometimes human beings are annoyed by Him because His heat is simply overbearing.

In Northern climates, however, the Sun reigns Supreme. In those cultures, rituals performed to illustrate the Sun's effect on the Earth usually coincide with the Sun's increase at the Solstice. Although they vary from country to country, most rituals are designed to celebrate the erotic fulfillment of Summer, to placate the Sun, and to extract from Him a promise to return again.

Japan holds the Lily Festival. On June 17, seven young women dressed in white robes make an offering of mountain lilies in a Shinto ceremony. The flowers remain on the altar overnight. The next day they are used by women in a dance to dispel the negative spirits of the rainy season, and a large float of these lilies is paraded through town to purify the air.

In Sweden the festival of Midsommar is celebrated on June 20. On this day the Swedes decorate their buildings, cars, and public facilities with birch twigs. Each town adorns a Maypole with wreaths and garlands of flowers. People dress in costumes and dance around the pole all night long.

The erotic promise of the Spring Maiden is fulfilled in the Bride of Summer, and in northern Europe a nubile young woman is chosen to represent the Goddess as she chooses a bridegroom.

115

Summer

These two are representative of the interaction between the Earth and the Sun, and the success or failure of the crops depends on their ritual performance.

In France and Spain lovers give each other a rose in a book. The erotic fulfillment of Nature is celebrated with carnivals, parades, and dancing in the streets.

In Eastern Europe girls weave nine kinds of flowers into a garland that they wear on their heads or legs overnight, hoping to dream of their future love. Sometimes candles are placed in the garland. The candles are lit and set afloat in a river. The lucky boy who retrieves this Ring of Fire is assured of love throughout the coming year.

When the Christian church usurped this holiday, the romantic symbolism was separated from the Goddess and relegated to the June bride. The tradition of the bride throwing the bridal bouquet originated as the tossing of the garland. And throwing rice at newlyweds reminds us of the couple's relationship to the harvest.

Placation of the Sun was an important feature of the Midsummer ritual. A bonfire was lit and numerous offerings were tossed into it with prayers to the Sun. Wooden wheels or barrels were set ablaze and rolled downhill to imitate the decrease of the Sun's light that would begin after the turn of the Solstice. It was believed that by making offerings and enacting the Sun's dance across the heavens, human beings could gain audience with the old man and extract from Him a promise to return after the darkness of the Winter Solstice.

The Summer Solstice actually occurs in the astrological month of Cancer (the Crab), the water element, which is ruled by the Moon. But the qualities of the Sun are attributed to the next sign in the astrological progression, the Fire sign of Leo the Lion. In the Western world the lion is thought of as the "king of the jungle" probably because his color and mane are reminiscent of a blazing Sun. In mythology the cultural hero often subdues a lion, and a brave man is referred to as "lionhearted." Leo is Sun-ruled, masculine, and courageous.

But the Sun is not always masculine, according to the mythology of various cultures:

> In Egypt the Goddess Hathor is addressed as "the Fiery One, She who was never created." In Arabia She is called Attar or Al-Ilat, Torch of the Gods. The Sun Goddess is named Anyanwu by the Ibo of Nigeria and "Indombe, the blazing heat" in Zaire. Akewa is Her name among the Toba people of Argentina. And the rising Sun, "the ruler of all the deities," is the Goddess Amaterasu of Japan. Oshun, the Yoruba river maiden, is the daughter of the Sun, and Mary, the Mother of Jesus, is the "woman clothed with the sun" (Revelations 12:1). She is Surma to the Celts, and to the Inuit (Eskimos) She is Sun Sister, who took to the heavens after being molested by Her brother the Moon.

> —Luisah Teish

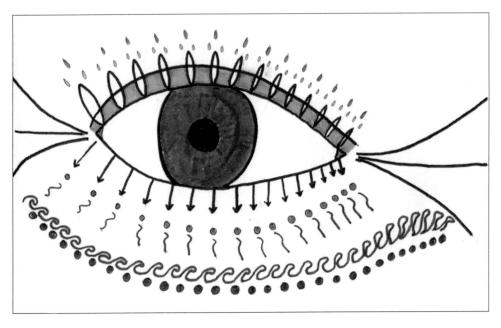

Hathor, the Fiery One, She who was never created.

It is safer to say that the Celestial Twins carry out the dual role of heating and cooling the Earth. The Sun gives soil, plant, animal, and human life the energy to expand and work, and the Moon gives us the opportunity and environment to contract and to rest.

Juneteenth

A few of the Midsummer events celebrate "the flame" as political power and divine inspiration. Most people are familiar with the Fourth of July, which celebrates American independence. But that independence occurred on the shoulders of slavery. "Juneteenth" is the Celebration of African American Independence. On June 19, 1865, news of the Emancipation Proclamation reached the ears of slaves on the plantations of Texas and Louisiana. The document had been signed in 1863, but this information was withheld for two years. Imagine being acquitted of a crime or released by law and being kept a prisoner for another two years! It's unspeakable. The end of slavery brought great rejoicing and fulfilled the prophecy of many plantation visionaries that "the freedom come" soon.

Today, Juneteenth is celebrated throughout the United States. It not only commemorates the liberation of the slaves but also honors the contributions that African Americans have made to the world. These celebrations usually take place on picnic grounds and include historical theater, a parade, and a baseball game. Because the information was withheld we are not sure of the exact date the news arrived in any given community, so Juneteenth is celebrated between the 13th and the 19th of the month.

St. John's Eve and St. John's Day

He must increase, but I must decrease.

—John the Baptist

The Church has masculinized the story of Jesus and his cousin

John the Baptist by not including the important presence of two women—their mothers—in their relationship.

In most Euro-American countries, June 24 is the Feast of Saint John the Baptist. Generally, the Catholic Church recognizes the death days of its saints as holy because their acts of martyrdom are revered and their entry into heaven is assumed to have occurred on that day. But John stands out as the exception to this rule. His birthday is considered important because of the folklore surrounding his mother, Elizabeth, who was a cousin of Mary the Virgin. The story goes like this:

> John was the issue of two righteous people, Zachary, a lawyer, and the virtuous Elizabeth. His father was doing the honor given him of lighting incense on the communal altar when he received a visit from the angel Gabriel. Gabriel told Zachary that Elizabeth would conceive and give birth to a son in spite of the fact that her fertile days had passed. Elizabeth, conceiving as a postmenopausal woman, can be seen as the Moon moving from dark to young crescent, the Crone renewing Herself as Maiden Mother.
>
> The old man was further informed that this boy would be "the morning star to usher in the Sun of justice and the Light of the World." When Zachary questioned the angel, he was struck dumb and remained so until the day the baby was born.
>
> Cousin Mary the Virgin, who was carrying her own miracle baby at the time, visited Elizabeth. It is said that when Elizabeth heard Mary's greeting, the baby jumped in her womb. And it is

believed that at that moment the divine light of grace was exchanged between the two infants. This day, known as the Visitation of Our Lady, has been celebrated since the fourteenth century on or near July 2. At this time, a statue of the Virgin is paraded through town as devotees appeal to Her for grace.

According to custom John was circumcised on the eighth day. Ordinarily he would have been named after his father, but the old man wrote on a tablet his wish to name the child John, and, upon doing so, not only did he regain his speech, but he also instantly composed and recited the *Benedictus*. This prayer is often recited by devotees and is especially appropriate at funerals.

A taboo against drinking liquor was imposed upon John from birth. With his sobriety assured, he grew up to become the author of his Gospels and the famed Baptist who washed his cousin, the Christ, in the river.[5]

John, like Joseph, is beloved of the common people. His feast day is celebrated by retaining the symbolism of the Summer Solstice.

St. John's Eve in New Orleans

By the 1800s, the Catholic Church had long before taken over the original European pagan holidays and turned them into saints' days. And now, European colonists were invading the North American continent (Turtle Island) and were busily exploiting its natural resources while systematically eliminating the original caretakers of the land, the Native American people. The slave traders brought Nature-worshiping people from the forests of equatorial Africa and placed them on the tobacco, sugar cane, and cotton plantations of the South. In their Motherland, these people had entertained a host of deities and ancestral spirits. They had developed a liturgical theater of magnificent music and dance and were educated about life from an oral tradition rich in folkloric characters. On the plantation these people found themselves in a very different cultural climate but were able to bring their unique flavor to the soup even under severely oppressive conditions.

The culture of New Orleans in the 1800s was European (French-Spanish-English), African (Dahomean-Congolese), and Native American (Choctaw). One of the main ingredients in the culture of New Orleans was the presence of Voudou, as dramatized by the Queen Mother, Mam'zelle Marie La Veau. She and her daughters did much to unify the women of New Orleans, Black and White, rich and poor, pagan and Christian.

Congo Square was "the Apollo" of New Orleans—the place where the best Voudou dancing in town could be witnessed. These dances were often raided by the police during a long political campaign against African religion that ravaged the city between 1820 and 1860. The Black Codes regulated the lives of Louisiana slaves and attempted to suppress the social and spiritual life of the free *gens de couleur* (people of color). But the dances in Congo Square were performances staged for the benefit of the disrupters. The real ceremonies were conducted from Mam'zelle's cabin at

Bayou St. John. And, according to local folklore, it was there that she held her annual Midsummer Feast on June 24, the Eve of St. John.

Congo Square

Saunter down old Rampart Street
Stop, inhale the air;
Tip your hat to good St. Anne
Then enter Congo Square.
Raise your left foot lightly;
Three times lay it down,
Bend your knees so slightly now
To kiss the hallowed ground.

Look upon your kindred, child',
The rocks, the trees, the birds;
Speak to them all silently,
The River's voice is heard.
There the spirits whisper
Here the dead are fair.
Now the Great Zombie appears
In the circle in Congo Square.
Below the green grass trembles,
Above, the full moon sings,
Spirit moves both in and out,
Between and through all things.

A cheese-box drum is played now,
With the jawbone of an ass.
Women don their finest whites,
Some slaves, some upper class.

Brick dust marks the circle
Red against black earth;
White clay marks the brow bone
Of the one marked for rebirth.
There's taffia and water,
And feathers stained with blood.
River spirits dance and drink
For heat, drought, and flood.

All the men are agile
All the women fair,
All the spirits leap and run
'Round the circle in Congo Square.

Piled high, wood is burning,
Black cauldron filled with oil.
The faithful step forth bravely,
While the charlatans recoil.
Now is the magic moment
The test of truth is here.
Only the devoted plunge their hands
In the pot of oil without fear.

Those who pass have honor.
Those who fail must go.
Only true believers pass
The test of Hunzi Canzo.

The spirits hover low now,
The people shout and dance,
The serpent wraps himself around
The queen in her proud prance.
She showers all with blessings
"La Reine de Jardiniere"
Mam'zelle La Veau frees all the slaves
In the circle in Congo Square.

All the trees are swaying
As warm gulf breezes blow,
And spores are gently landing
Where Spanish moss will grow.

All the Men are howling
As all the women flirt.
Toil and tears with blood and rum
Sink down into the dirt.

Then all the joy is fractured
When cannon's boom is heard.
And so, the dance must end now.

125

As the Law has sent the word.
And all the people exit
And scatter everywhere,
Taking the magic with them,
Leaving shadows in Congo Square.

But from the Square they venture
To the house on old S. Anne;
Or, behind the doors of "La Maison Blanche"
Mam'zelle unfolds her plan.

Inside she shelters runaways,
Takes poor girls off the street.
She purifies and teaches them,
In a manner most discreet.
The queen will soon adorn them
And start the Quadroon Ball.
She'll mate them there through Le Placage
Behind her cottage walls.

Their children will be born there,
The old and sick will heal.
Her gumbo, sent to those condemned,
Gives death a peaceful meal.
And when the slaves revolted
Against their wretched lot,

Mam'zelle Marie is found to be
The mistress of the plot.

She listens to the stories
The upper crust has told
Then turns the tales against them
In a manner brave and bold.
She could kill or cure with plants,
With thought or with a Hand.
She know the herbs of Africa,
Of Haiti, and this land.

Men of high class loved her
Some came from far away.
Rumor says she received a shawl
From the emperor of China one day.
We know of Square and cottage
Yet mysteries remain
Deep in the waters of Bayou St. John
And the waters of Pontchartrain.

For there they walked through fire,
Danced on water and through the air,
Performing the ancient African rites
Never seen in Congo Square.

—Luisah Teish (taken from *Heritage of Power* by Susheel Bibbs)

127

Summer

Dancing and Singing with Saint John

There were several dances performed for the Solstice. Some, like the Calinda, were mating dances wherein men and woman made flirtatious gestures to each other. Other versions, done by the men, included a combination of movements retained from an African style of stick fighting that is still practiced in Trinidad today. The men fought, bare chested, while balancing bottles of water on their heads; the man who spilled his water was the loser. Now, it is interesting to note that the men fought while balancing water on their heads, because in the St. John's Eve ceremony in New Orleans, Mam'zelle Marie emerged from the waters of Lake Pontchartrain balancing burning candles on her head. This practice is reminiscent of the European Luciadagen, when a young woman balanced a crown of lit candles on her head to honor the Sun.

The songs that accompanied these dances had much in common with the Trinidadian calypso. Often the songs appear to speak of seasonal celebrations and sensuous lovemaking, but they also addressed political injustice and contained a call to acts of rebellion both great and small. Practically every city official found himself the subject of one of these songs, and slave women used the songs to declare themselves smarter and prettier than their mistresses. The Solstice dance celebrated the strength of the Sun and the sweetness of fresh water, and the songs were used for fighting and loving.

The ceremonies at Bayou St. John could go on late into the night; but in the Square, when the 9 o'clock cannon was fired in the Place d'Armes, the Sun went down for those who wore black skin and the slavers' brand. And the soup lost its flavor until they returned. Rituals similar to those practiced in old New Orleans live on in the islands of Puerto Rico, Trinidad, and Togo. But the customs of St. John's Day predate slavery and Christianity. At its root it is primarily a celebration of the Divine Couple, of Isis and Osiris, of the balance between Fire and Water.

Initiation into the Temple of the Sun

In the Summer of 1969 I was initiated in the Fahamme Temple of Amun-Ra in St. Louis, Missouri. The Reverend Paul Nathaniel Johnson founded the temple in 1927. I give praise and thanks to Rev. Johnson and my initiator, Sheikh Ankhnaten, who are both ancestors now.

My initiation was an eighteen-hour process. I loved the intellectual stimulation of the service, but it had little music and no dance directly connected to it, and I longed for these. When I'd successfully completed this ordeal, I was given my current name, Luisah Teish, which means "Adventuresome Spirit." I became the child of the Divine Couple: Isis, the Mother of Mystery, and Osiris, the Powerful Sun.

Temple membership required that we commit to study, observe certain taboos, and embrace the Fahamme point of view. I studied the principles of metaphysics, symbology, numerology, and astrology. An Imam of the temple introduced me to the idea of science

129

fiction as spiritual revelation of the future. As a child I'd read Greek and Roman mythology because they were the only mythologies available to me, but now, in the temple, I was introduced to Egyptian mythology and to the family of Isis. Temple members observed fasting as a health measure and observed periods of silence for mental balance. We abstained from eating scavengers (including pork, shrimp, and crab), and we maintained cleanliness of body and environment. We also studied the martial arts and supported each other in business. And, we prayed daily.

But the most important teaching was about Understanding. Initiates were advised to practice their own tradition but also to seek to understand every tradition. The elders said that Understanding enriched the mind and empowered the spirit. I took this teaching very seriously, and it nurtured in me a hunger for culture that guides my life to this day.

My elders in the Fahamme temple maintained that Egypt was the land of Black people in predynastic times. But Eurocentric education consistently annexed Egypt to a place called "the Middle East." Whenever I looked at a map, Egypt was right there on the African continent. In college, anthropologists boggled my mind by insisting that although most of the people of Egypt had black skin, they "weren't really Black." They claimed that there were many similarities between the Egyptians and the Greeks but no similarities between Egyptians and sub-Saharan Africans. But this point of view conflicted with the biological evidence that the entire human race originated in Black Africa. I decided to reject these contradictions and accepted kinship with Egyptians as an act of common sense. But still I wondered what the Egyptians themselves thought and felt.

At that time, I wanted to travel to Egypt, thinking that then I'd have the opportunity to find out for myself, but before I went to Egypt, I found myself back in Hawaii. . . .

Return to the Goddess Pele

I timed my Hawaiian vacation to arrive in Hilo during the week of the Indigenous People's Conference because I wanted to spend my Summer in "cultural heaven." In Hawaii, Paradise is guaranteed. I knew there would be sunshine and warm breezes, a mighty Ocean, and friendly tidepools. There'd be ginger and orchids, hibiscus and birds of paradise. There'd be fresh fish and boiled taro greens to eat, kava tea and pineapple-passionfruit juice to drink. There would be warm friendly people, sensuous music, and the sacred Hula dance. And most of all, there would be my sister Pele, the Sun in the belly of the Earth.

My luggage got lost at the airport and my reservations got misplaced. (Elegba, the Cross Master, lives.) But not to worry. I was welcomed and cared for by my sister-friend Halifu Osumare (whose name means "the arrow in the rainbow"), an African American woman who was doing her doctoral work at the University of Hawaii. Halifu took me home with her and chuckled softly as I marveled at the pineapple patch outside her kitchen window. Soon I'd taken to eating fresh fruit, talking to the birds in the trees, and napping in a chair on the porch. The jet lag got me. And so did the tropical breeze. I overslept the next morning and missed the Sunrise ceremony of the Indigenous Festival on the beach. By noon I made my way to the festival grounds where the Hula hilaus (hula schools) were performing their sacred dances.

I'd been to small resorts in Hawaii before, but this was my first time at an Indigenous Festival. Now I could really feel the Spirit of the people. Now I could imagine what life in an early (precolonial) village must have been like. The grass-roofed longhouses, the open field of people, the strong sense of community, the drums, the dance. . . . It felt like Africa . . . only cooler. I went to the flower market to buy tapa cloth and flowers, then sat quietly to wait for my sister-friend.

Several people came up to me and asked, "Auntie, what island are you from?" (Some thought I was Samoan.) I'd respond, "I live on the mainland, but Africa is my home." A few people sat to talk awhile. I learned that they were Native American, Sami, and Maori. Everyone was friendly, everyone sincere. I drifted the days away by soaking in clear water, eating sweet fruit, and listening to music. Too soon, my time in Hawaii would draw to a close. I had to go face Pele, the Queen of the flame.

So there I stood, happy yet trembling, with my Ti leaf offering in my hand. Talking to the deep crater in the mountain.

I know from experience that I must be careful of what I ask for; I've learned to be mindful of what I say. For Pele's way is sud-

den and furious; it is all-consuming and profoundly transformative. Do I need more passion? More courage? More strength?

I lifted the offering up to my lips and whispered, "O Pele O, my
sister . . . I'm cool."

from Celebration of the Moon to Celebration of the Sun

In Egyptian mythology Isis, the Queen of Heaven, and Her
brother-lover Osiris, are credited with a prosperous dual rulership
over the land. Under their balanced guidance the arts and sciences
flourished. The people learned to chart the stars and predict the
weather, fashion tools, cultivate crops, build cities, weave cloth, and
spin magic. Lower Egypt (in the north) and Upper Egypt (in the
south) were autonomous city-states. The culture was sensuous and
strongly matriarchal, with women holding positions of power in
every stratum of the society.

Isis is envisioned as a slender and beautiful woman standing
erect, moving in procession, kneeling with Vulture wings
extended, or sitting on a throne holding Her son, Horus. In fact,
Isis *is* the throne upon which the pharaohs of Egypt sat. Her
crown, a solar or lunar disc centered in an impressive pair of horns,
symbolizes Her connection to both Heaven and Earth.

The worship of Isis of the Thousand Breasts originated in
Egypt and spread to the Greek and Roman worlds. Known by
many names, She is called Panthea, the All Goddess; Khut, the

Light Giver; Renenet, the Harvest Queen, the Lady of Abundance, Beauty, and Bread; Placidea Reginae, the Queen of Peace; Sesheta, the Lady of Literature; Sophia, the Divine Wisdom; Medicina Mundi, the Medicine That Heals the World; and Venerandum, She Who Must Be Adored. The active veneration of Isis survived Christian persecution well into the sixth century and began to be revived worldwide during the twentieth century. (For more information, contact the Federation of Isis, Enniscorthy, Ireland.) The most popular myth about her celebrates the mystery of the Death and Resurrection of her brother-husband Osiris. Here is the short version:

> Isis and Osiris became lovers, married, and initiated a peaceful and prosperous civilization and culture. Harmony in Egypt depended on the movement of Sothis (the Dog Star Sirius) and the flooding of the Nile. This flooding watered the fields and produced crops, and such abundance was celebrated with joyous festivals.
>
> Once, while traveling east (to India or China maybe), Osiris was called by his brother, Set, to return home. Set threw a big party upon Osiris' return, and, as entertainment, He introduced an elaborately carved box (sounds like a coffin to me). Set made a game of "Who can fit in the box?" and of course only Osiris fit perfectly. Set and his posse promptly closed the box and threw it in the Nile. It was carried away until it rested in the trunk of a tamarisk tree. (Doesn't this remind you of the story of Moses?)

When Isis heard the news of Her lover's predicament She called on Anubis, the Dog of the Underworld, to assist Her in the search. They found the tree just as the King of Byblus was cutting it down to make a column for his palace. Isis changed Herself into a dove (She should have tried the vulture and intimidation) and pleaded with the King to spare the tree, but to no avail. So She changed Herself back into a woman and took a job as the King's nursemaid. She befriended the household servants and secured the coffin of Her beloved. Set got word of Her victory and stole the coffin back from Her. He dismembered Osiris into fourteen pieces and scattered them over the land. Then Isis performed a miracle.

Isis had the task of finding each piece. With her sister Nephthys and her nephew Anubis she traveled far and wide until she had located every piece except the phallus. This had been eaten ... by a spider. She then made a phallic likeness from wood and brought the whole body to Abydos for burial.

Together with Nephthys, her sister, Anubis, her nephew, and Thoth, her uncle, Isis wept bitterly over her dead husband and chanted magically. So powerful were the tears and prayers and the occult powers of Thoth that the penis of Osiris began to evidence vitality and secured conception for the faithful wife. Osiris then ascended to Heaven, from which sublime place he continued to watch over Isis while she carried and bore his only son, Horus.[6]

Then everything got turned around.

135

After the invasion of Egypt by Indo-Europeans circa 3000 B.C., Lower and Upper Egypt were united under a newly instituted kingship, and the Dynastic Era began. The invaders, calling themselves the "Followers of Horus," formed an aristocracy, or master race, that ruled over Egypt. The word *pharaoh* (*par-o* means simply "great house") was applied to the royal male alone.

Egypt lost its balance under this military dictatorship. The priesthood became an exclusive brotherhood, and "the male governors of Egyptian dynasties now pretended to have been created by a father God. He, Ptah, was supposed to have created the other gods through an act of masturbation."[7]

The Great Goddess Isis, the "Golden One," was demoted to Madonna, the Mother of Horus; Osiris, the Moon God, became associated with the Sun; and the calendar was changed from lunar to solar.

The story of Isis has some features in common with that of Mary. She gives birth to the Divine Child as Mary does. The fundamental difference lies in the fact that Isis is allowed to be sexual, and that sexual power produces Life from Death. Isis and Osiris are depicted as true romantics, as devoted lovers, but it should be known that Isis also had another husband, Min.

The Summer Calendar

Originally, the Egyptian calendar consisted of twelve months. Each month contained three ten-day weeks. A season was regarded as containing four such months, and there were three seasons to the year (30 x 4 = 120 days x 3 = 360 days).

The additional five days that give us our year of 365 days were acquired by the act of magic, a game of chance.

The movement of the star Sirius, which the Egyptians identified with Isis, determined the calendar. The Summer Solstice occurred in the eleventh calendar month, when Sirius rose in the constellation Orion, Leo the Lion. Osiris was believed to reside in that constellation, and the Divine Couple was celebrated at that time. The stellar bodies of Isis and Osiris would appear on the horizon just before sunrise in mid-June. Then the waters of the Nile would begin to swell, flow over their banks, and fertilize the valley. And as the Lily of the Nile blossomed and beautified life on Earth, people lifted their faces to the Sun and celebrated the Summer Solstice.

Suggestions for Celebrating Summer

I am a storyteller and often perform for elementary school kids. My repertoire contains several stories with stellar themes. "Why the Sun and the Moon Live in the Sky" and "How We Got the Wishing Star" are two of the children's favorites. After a small in-class session, I give the kids drawing paper and crayons and ask them to draw me a picture of the story. Over the years I've noticed that many children will include a rainbow in their picture even though there was no rainbow in the story. Perhaps they can see something that we can't!

Not a Cloud in the Sky

You may want to try this little exercise with your kids while on a picnic at the beach or in the park. Set them up with crayons and paper in a comfortable place. Ask them to close their eyes and visualize the clouds in the sky. With their eyes closed have them draw the cloud that they see in their vision. Then have them open their eyes and look at the clouds in the sky. Now have them close their eyes again, and this time ask them to draw the cloud shape they just saw in the sky. Now have them open their eyes and look for the cloud they just saw. No doubt it will have changed its shape a bit. Do this a few times.

Then ask them to make up a story about the shapes they saw in the clouds. You'll be amazed by what they come up with.

The Seasonal Altar or Table

Place three candles—red, orange, and yellow; or silver, white, and gold—in a large glass bowl of water scented with your favorite oil. Name the candles for Isis, Osiris, and Horus, or for Sun, Moon, and clouds. Select three people—a woman, a man, and a youth—to light the candles. With each lighting, make a petition to the flame. For example, ask the Sun to shine mercifully for the sake of the flowers, ask the Moon to grace the night sky for storytelling, ask the clouds to send a gentle rain. This circle of light can be used as the center of the seasonal altar or the dinner table for a Summer meal.

A Summer Ritual

This ritual is ideally done at the Summer Solstice.

To *vacate,* part of the word *vacation,* means to "empty out." In Summer, whether on vacation or not, we can take advantage of the transformative power of Fire by surrendering our concerns to the all-consuming flame. The ritual that follows is best done outside around an open fire. It may also be done indoors using a cauldron or some other fire-safe metal container.

Preparation

You will need:

Firewood

A cauldron or other fire-safe metal container (if you do the ritual indoors)

Paper and matches for starting the fire

Pen and paper for writing

A handful of grain such as corn, wheat, or millet

A bowl of water with a flower floating in it

Invoking the Directions

Invoke the directions by visualizing the image described for each and speaking the image out loud so that others may share in the vision. Call the energy in Nature to you, and call the energy to awaken within you. At the end of each invocation instruct the family to regard the next direction.

East: In the East we call upon the power of the Rising Sun, the yellow light of the morning. Here we ask for new beginning, and we commit to renewing ourselves.

South: In the South we call upon the power of the Sun at High Noon, the bright, orange light that warms the day. Here we ask for strength to be with us, and we commit to using our strength for the good of the community.

West: In the West we call upon the power of the Setting Sun, the deep red light that calms the mind at the end of the day. Here we ask for a sense of satisfaction, and we pledge to take care of ourselves.

North: In the North we call upon the power of the Moon in the Night Sky, the silvery Moon who permits us to rest. Here we ask for the vision of dreams, and we agree to meet our ancestors in that place.

Be sure to close the directions at the end of the ritual by moving counter-clockwise, thanking each direction for its energy.

Performing the Ritual

Sit or stand in a circle around the fire. Take nine slow, deep breaths with eyes closed. See the light of the fire through your closed eye-lids.

Sit quietly with pen and paper. Write down all the mistakes, regrets, doubts, and, especially, fears that you may be holding inside. Fold the paper from the bottom up, moving it away from you as you fold it. At your will, toss this paper into the flame and watch the smoke rise.

Turn your back to the flame for a few minutes while you speak your hopes and desires into a handful of grain. Breathe deeply. Toss the grain into the flame over your left shoulder.

Now turn around and look at the flame.

Pass the bowl of water with the flower floating in it around the circle. Now each person should close their eyes again long enough to anoint the left, right, and third eye with water. Remove the flower and toss the water into the fire. Watch the steam that appears. Now each person can take a petal from the flower to carry in his or her purse or pocket for wish fulfillment.

A Summer Recipe: A Little Something Cool

I grew up with Southern hospitality, which required that anyone approaching the house in Summer must be offered "a little something to cool your thirst" before we could talk. Sometimes that "something" was a frosty root beer, other times it was a spicy iced tea, but most often it was good old-fashioned lemonade.

In my lifetime I've taken to a few addictions: beautiful books, international fabrics, exotic flowers, and tropical fruit juices and

141

Summer

teas. I always try to keep something chilling in the fridge, and, thanks to California cuisine, I have many options. Depending upon where you live, you may want to store large quantities of "a little something cool" in your refrigerator. Here are a few suggestions:

Mix two parts orange-pineapple, orange-tangerine, or orange-mango juice in a pitcher with one part mineral water. Squeeze the juice of one small lemon and add it to the mixture. Let it chill and serve.

Steep a pot of mango-peach, wild forest blackberry, or hibiscus tea. Add honey while still hot. Dissolve the honey. Let the tea cool. Add lemon juice and small bits of fresh mint leaf. Pour this over crushed ice and sip it with a straw.

Play with other combinations. They're all cool.

Autumn

A Personal Encounter with Autumn: Going Crazy in Caracas

I love the mountains and flowers.

I love the sky and the trees.

I love the music, the food,

And the people,

But the traffic in Caracas makes me crazy.

These are the words I chanted every day during my stay in the beautiful country of Venezuela.

I'd been invited to perform by La Casa de la Poesia, the International Poetry House in Caracas. My hotel room was pretty and peaceful, and the food was plentiful and close at hand. My host family were more than gracious hosts; they were family. So everything was fine until I had to face the traffic. Cars were going everywhere, and they were going all the time. This was so different from Hawaii, from where I had just come. To me the traffic seemed to be as fast as Germany's, as crowded as New York's, and as hostile and dangerous as that in Lagos and Los Angeles. Since I couldn't navigate my way across the street, I was reluctant to go anywhere at all.

145

Autumn

A courageous young man, a son of Shango, agreed to be my personal bodyguard. It made me feel safe and secure. (*Gracias, Santito.*) We took a ride in the countryside, my favorite place in anybody's country. We stopped along the road to pick flowers, to play with parrots, and of course to savor the local food. It was there that I fell in love with *arepas,* a kind of "mooncake" made from whole-kernel yellow corn.

After a pilgrimage to the shrine of the local Goddess (we'll go there together later), we returned to the city and prepared to go to work. I held a two-day workshop "for women only," which brought a lot of questions from the media and a lot of women to the workshop. We managed to overcome the language barrier. I needed two interpreters for the spoken word and two translators of the written word. The only thing missing was a sign-language interpreter for the hearing impaired, but we didn't need it this time.

In the evenings the theater filled with people. Poetry is the "popular voice of the people" in South America, and the poets are very fine. There were poets from countries on every continent. Many were from various parts of South America and Europe, a few were from Asia and Australia, and there was an African man from Benin.

One night a magnificent thing happened: The African man read his poetry in Bendel (the language of Benin) and French, and then he passed it to a man who read it in Italian, who passed it to a man who read it in Spanish. I waited for the English version, but it never came. At that moment I realized that I was the only American, the only native English speaker, and the only person in the house with minimal language skills in any nonnative tongue. I remembered the debate over bilingual education in California schools and felt myself at a disadvantage. I made a note to Elegba to remind me to take out my foreign language programs and put them in the computer when I got home. Someone was kind enough to tell me that the African man's poem was in honor of the ancestors, and that it was a beautiful one at that.

The next night I gave a performance in English with a translator who marveled at my ability to say things in Black English that "couldn't really be said in Spanish." But again I realized during the show that most of the audience knew English very well, and they had learned Black English from the lyrics of American music on the radio.

I had come to Caracas for poetry and a pilgrimage, and I got that and so much more.

Crazy in Caracas

Perhaps it was the mountain
Or the blue sky up above.
It could have been
The great green trees
That made me fall in love.

I watched the purple sunsets

Through sheets of sweet
Soft rain.
I sighed and slept
And when
I rose,
I fell in love again.

It could have been
The poetry,
The food,
The song,
The dance.
Or could it be
The spirits here
Are given to romance?

And to this day
I still can't say
Just when the cool wind blew.
I lost the mind
I still can't find.
Oh dear, what shall I do?
—Luisah Teish

An Introduction to Autumn: Goddess of the Winds of Change

Softly a whistle rises in the wind, gently the dust broom sweeps. Leaves rustle against the Earth. Oya, Queen of the Winds of Change, rises, growing stronger, standing taller, pushing farther, yielding more. Long and swift She dances through our lives, hurling lightning and spitting fire while furiously torrential rains fall. We reap the harvest. We grab the shafts of wheat and rip them from the soil. Oya, Mother of Transformation—we work so well for Her.

Oya, Lady of the Sunset, paints the leaves in Autumn. The hum of locusts is Her song. There in the cemetery She dances among the

It could have been the poetry, the food, the song, the dance....

tombstones with Her Sisters at Her side. There in Her garden, leaves and seeds fly while rain falls upon the Earth. Death and Life rustle in the Wind, the seasons change, and we who are the Dead-reborn must worship Her.

On the Summer Solstice we enjoyed the longest day of the year. The next day, the Sun began to decrease its light, moving ever closer to Autumn. On Earth we live by the grace of the Sun's interaction with our planet. And so we live in anticipation of the movements that will give us the Harvest. In some communities the celebrations begin weeks before the actual Equinox.

On September 4, some Native North Americans celebrate a Sunrise Dance. At this time of the year White Mountain Apache maidens adorn themselves in buckskin and feathers in honor of Changing Woman. Their fathers shower them with corn kernels and candy as a protection against famine.

In India, the Hindu Elephant God, Ganesh, is celebrated on September 5. He represents wisdom, wealth, and humor. At this time He is decorated and given His favorite food offerings to assure a bountiful kitchen.

September 7 is the day that Cuba satisfies the Water women with the Feast of Yemaya and Oshun. They are the sisters of Oya, the Queen of the Winds of Change. On this day devotees celebrate the Goddess of the Ocean and the Queen of the River with elaborate altars, fine foods, and a procession.

In Switzerland, on September 14, a statue of the Black Madonna is adorned with flowers and paraded through town. Then She is left at a roadside shrine where offerings of food and fire are made to Her.

Naturally, we associate such celebrations with farming communities, where people are bound to the land. But even desert nomads celebrate a harvest. The Tuareg and Wodaabe people of northern Niger celebrate the Cure Saleé on September 11. After the first rains of the season they celebrate the salt contained in the new grass, which is essential for the camel's diet. They gather to sing, dance, share food, and hold camel races. (I'll tell all about those camels later.)

And in Egypt the mysterious lady Nephthys, the Revealer, the Sister of Isis, hosts a fire ceremony. Candles and lanterns are placed before Her to lead us into the light and to reveal that which is hidden.

The Autumn Equinox

The Autumn Equinox is the time of perfect balance between day and night, dark and light. Here the astrological sign Libra, the Scales balancing Justice and Mercy, symbolizes the equilibrium of the Celestial Couple.

The harvest associated with the Equinox has been observed by people all over the world since the advent of agriculture. There are many customs. The plants were personified as Corn Mother, Wheat Woman, Lady Rye, and Harvest Queen, and Her consort was the Green Man, the Grain King, and the Sun-Father. People approached the Harvest with deep solemnity and joyous celebration. To emphasize Continuous Creation, soil or seed from this year's harvest was often kept through the Winter and mixed with the Spring planting. Quite simply, people everywhere marked the

151

Autumn

time when the crops were harvested, because this meant that the work in the garden was finished for that year.

Soon the barren roots were ripped from the ground. These roots were rolled and twisted into wreaths, embellished with dried flowers, and hung on the door of the house to symbolize the cyclical nature of the seasons. The food would be preserved and stored as security against the scarcity of Winter. For a while, the garden would lie fallow while the Earth regenerated Her energy in the seasonal cycle. This practice also reflected a belief about human existence, namely, that the body, like the husk of the corn, dies and falls away, but the Spirit, like the seed, is reborn. All peoples held beliefs such as this.

The Harvest Moon is the Full Moon that occurs closest to the Autumn Equinox. Usually it looms so large in the Oakland sky that I imagine I could just leap into it and bounce right back. Harvest Moon is the time when we gather the crops, cure the seeds for planting, and store grain to secure ourselves against the trial of Winter.

The period between September 15 and 30 is held in high regard in many countries. It is a time to celebrate the harvesting of staple crops, such as yams in West Africa, the sacred corn of the Native American, rice in China, and the ever-popular pumpkin.

The African Yam festival and Native American Corn Rituals

The African yam is a large, porous tuber with white flesh and coarse skin. It is often pounded into flour, boiled, and mashed into mush for *fu fu* (dumplings), or subjected to herbal compounds and incantations to become medicine and food of the Gods.

The first yams of the harvest are always offered to the ancestors and the deities in ceremonies that include singing, dancing, and storytelling; libations of rum, wine, or water; and the lighting of ritual fires. Although the specifics of the ritual may differ from one country or region to the next, certain beliefs are held in common by all peoples of the West African diaspora. These include a belief that the yam contains some of the Spirit of the ancestors; that it is a gift from the Earth; that it can impart to its consumer virtues such as patience and humility; and that, if not properly respected and celebrated, it will cease to be, causing famine, poverty, and numerous other ills. After proper ritual, the spirits and the human community share the yams. September 15-20 marks the celebration of the Yam Festival in West Africa and in the African cultures of the Caribbean.

Native Americans regard corn with the same great reverence as Africans do the yam. It is a gift of Life from the Corn Mother and is celebrated in a number of rituals. Often it is smoked overnight in a hole in the Earth. Song and prayer accompany this ritual. The husks are used not only for wrapping food and other personal items but also for creating ancestral dolls.

A gift of life from the Corn Mother.

Mooncakes and Hungry Ghosts

At the Harvest Moon in China, rice and wheat are harvested and made into large, round "mooncakes." These are presented along with offerings of melons and pomegranates to the Goddess Chang

Goddess Chang O, the Lady in the Harvest Moon.

O, the Lady in the Moon. The women who make these cakes whisper secret wishes into them. The cakes represent harmony and unity within the family. Also at this celebration a young girl is chosen to enter "the heavenly gardens," where she has visions of the future prosperity of the community. The night is spent playing games of fortune and rejoicing under the Light of the Moon.

Halloween

Growing up in New Orleans, I went to segregated schools. The students, teachers, and administrators were all varying shades of Black. Yet my elementary school textbooks were all about young White children. That's right—I was taught to read with Dick and Jane.

Dick and Jane had many things that I did not have. They lived in a beautiful house. Their parents never fussed or fought. And they went to the ocean in the Summer. But most important, Dick and Jane had Autumn. In their Autumn, red, orange, brown, and gold leaves fell from the trees, the children danced in the pumpkin patch, and windswept Sunday hats tumbled across the page. In their Autumn, Dick and Jane visited Plymouth Rock and played games like Pilgrims and Indians. My Autumn consisted of wind and rain; it lacked the brilliant colors of Dick's and Jane's New England Autumn. But my Autumn was special to me because we had the mystery and madness of Halloween, and Thanksgiving was the beginning of the deep cooking season when my relatives began their kitchen festival.

On Halloween night the entire neighborhood would make jack-o'-lanterns and set them on the banquette, in the window, or beside the screen door. This gave the neighborhood a warm eerie feeling, as if invaded by sinister watchmen with heads but no bodies. Children dressed in trick-or-treat costumes such as Frankenstein, the Wolfman, and various local demons who had crawled out of the swamp covered in slime and Spanish moss.

There was no need for parents to accompany their children because the parents who lived there supervised each block. In our neighborhood the tricks were harmless and the treats were sweet. People did not poison children's apples, and kids did not stray from the group. Each child was met at the door with a "Please don't get me, Mr. Wolfman" followed by praline candy and homemade tea-cakes. The children held open their bags to receive the treats, said hearty thank you's, and began trading goodies with each other as they headed for the next house. The door-to-door collections were usually over by 9 P.M., and then the feast of pumpkin pie and peach brandy would commence.

In my neighborhood there was a burly brown-skinned man; we'll call him Mr. Buck. Mr. Buck was generally a nice guy who loved to fish and hunt but who occasionally drank too much and displayed a twisted humor and disposition. One Halloween night he invited a group of us young trick-or-treaters to come inside his house. He asked us to wait in the living room while he went to the back, supposedly to refill the big bowl of candy from which he'd been serving his callers. We had waited for what seemed like a long time when suddenly Mr. Buck appeared in a white sheet with a rifle and a rope. We went into a profound hysteria and ran, stepping and stumbling over each other with tears streaming from our

Autumn

eyes. We ran from the house screaming, and the block guardians came running to investigate the matter. As we described what had come after us, Mr. Buck stood in his doorway laughing. The block mothers declared that he should be ashamed of himself, while the fathers warned him not to press his luck. Some of the kids described him as a ghost with a gun, but I knew he'd dressed in the cloak and hood of the Ku Klux Klan. Mr. Buck stands out as the most frightening trick of all time.

While Dick and Jane played Pilgrims and Indians, my mother reminded me that her mother was Choctaw and that it was "a shame before God" how the White folks had taken the Indians' land. She'd end with an admonition that "it don't pay to be nice to everybody."

With the passing of the years, Halloween became less and less important to me. In junior high I lost my interest in costumes and candy; the whole thing became silly, boring, and best left to children. By the time I was a senior in high school I'd learned to regard the seasons of Scorpio through Capricorn (October 24–January 19) with dread. It seemed to me that all my relatives, friends, and favorite people got sick, had accidents, or died during this time— especially the men in my life (son, uncle, lover). This still holds true for me today. Further, if these tragedies happened at any other time of the year, I seemed to remember and mourn during Scorpio. Later I realized that this was very appropriate behavior.

My sophomore year in college (1968) found me deeply involved in the struggle for Black Studies, fighting to learn and eat with no time for Halloween and other "White madness."

The Fahamme Temple shifted my attention away from Halloween completely. The temple members simply disregarded it. We focused on the Equinox with praises to Ra and remembrances of Isis's search for Osiris.

It was not until the 1980s, after several informative conversations with Starhawk, that I began to regard Halloween with understanding (as my Fahamme elders had instructed).

In San Francisco the sacredness of the season is overshadowed by the love of costume balls. But Starhawk explained that Hallomas is *more* than a costume ball. It is the time when Europeans celebrate their ancestors' return from the land of the dead. Since then I have attended several of her Hallomas ceremonies, where people rip their clothing and call the names of their dead relations. I've also come to understand that Hallomas marks the transition from the light half of the year to the dark. It is a time for Western culture to recognize ugliness, deformity, and death, a time for the culture to exorcise its collective shadow. These explanations gave Hallomas new meaning for me, and I began to celebrate it again in an attempt to bond with my pagan sisters.

Dia de los Muertos

Living in the San Francisco Bay Area has afforded me a rich spiritual and cultural life. I love to travel all over the world, and I am always happy to land here at home. There's so much magic here, and I have wonderful friends. I recall the first time I met Katarina one breezy Autumn evening when I was walking through the Mission District. Katarina was strolling down 24th Street wearing nothing but a short-strapped purse and a straw hat with a daisy in her hatband. She does this every year and gets away with it, intact. You see, Katarina is one of the many spirits who roam the streets of San Francisco on the Day of the Dead.

Día de los Muertos, November 1, is a magical night. People of Latin and Caribbean descent, and those with an affinity for the culture, decorate their homes with bright paper cutouts and dress their altars with candles and human skulls made of sugar and shiny colored foil. Some people paint their faces half-black and half-white and then parade in the streets playing drums and jumping up, while others offer flowers and sweet breads *(pan muerto)* to the spirits in the cemetery.

Oya is the Goddess of the Winds of Change. Although the Wind appears to be invisible, Her power is most obvious when it manifests as the tumultuous weather changes that occur in Autumn. By fanning Her skirt of Autumn leaves and dried palm fronds, Oya produces tornadoes, earthquakes, and hurricanes. She is the dutiful Mother of Catastrophe, the one who destroys out-worn structures and sweeps away debris. Coupled with this tem-pestuous Queen of Lightning is Her husband, Shango, the Lord of Thunder. Together they are the tropical storm that uproots the old structures, the rain that fertilizes the Earth, the great release of electrical energy that clears and cleans the atmosphere. It's said that

Oya married a fierce man, but She is fiercer than Her husband.

She is honored in Nigeria, the Caribbean, and Brazil. In Haiti She is known as Maman Brigitte, the wife of Baron Samedi and friend of Ghede-Nibo. There She has authority over the graves of women. In India She is feared and revered as Kali-Ma, the Mother of Destruction. She can be associated with the awesome Medusa and with Hecate of the Greeks. She is similar to Pele, Hawaii's Goddess of the Volcano. She is Coaticue of the Aztecs, wearing a skirt made of serpents and a necklace of hands and hearts. She's the One who raises the dust devil, causing whirlwinds and earthquakes with Her dance. She is also known as Changing Woman among Native North Americans. In the pantheon of the Egyptians She is Nephthys, the Revealer.

Fire, Wind, and Water—She is called by many names. Oya is the dark of the Moon, the Boss Lady of the Cemetery. When Her friend Iku (Death) visits, the last breath exhaled from the body is captured in Her winds. Then She takes the soul of the dead on Her wings and delivers it to the land of the ancestors.

Sometimes Katarina comes to see me. She walks right in and takes a front-row-center seat. She's here to see the *Masquerade Egungun* and to dance with the Goddess Oya.

Dancing with the Dead

During the Ancestral Season, which begins, generally, around October 18 and ends on November 2, my extended family honors the ancestors with a Masquerade Egungun. At the masquerade we dress up as family members or historical figures and portray the lives and deeds of those people in short dramatic presentations. We construct an altar to the Goddess Oya and surround Her with an entourage of ancestors. We hold special ceremonies for our own ancestors, with each ceremony reflecting the descendants' cultural background—African, Native American, Latin, or pre-Christian European. These feasts include decorative altars and elaborate meals with breads corresponding to the culture being honored—*pan muerto,* cornbread, *akara,* or *njeri.* Then we make a visit to the cemetery carrying "consecrated brooms." There we pick up debris, sweep, lay flowers, and say prayers for the spirits of those who have been neglected by their descendants.

Of course, during this time the rest of the neighborhood is celebrating with the standard "trick or treat." All the houses have jack-o'-lanterns or paper skeletons adorning their front doors. At my own home, I decorate the front porch with an Ancestral Harvest altar.

I drape a piece of cloth over the windows, set out a few tables and boxes of different heights, and cover them with cloth. I draw faces on the backs of four paper plates and tack them to the cloth in the North, South, East, and West positions. Then I dress the altar with numerous pumpkins of various sizes, squashes, gourds, ears of corn, yams, and the dried roots of plants pulled from my garden. Next I place several of the sugar skulls made especially for Día de los Muertos. Four small metal bowls are filled with soil, and orange, brown, green, and yellow candles (in their glasses) are secured in the soil. These serve as lamps for the altar. The whole thing is sprinkled with wild rice and red wine. As a finishing touch I stick nine pinwheels in the ground around the yard.

I've created this altar to remind people, visually, of the connection between the ancestors and the harvest. In recent years I've taken to stringing orange lights around the fence, and hanging glow-in-the-dark skeletons in the trees outside, with lizards and spiders, dinosaurs and snakes. There'll be more than enough ghouls and goblins in my neighbor's decorations. And so, I dedicate my yard to keeping the connection between Nature and the ancestors. At this time of year, when all the ancestors are roaming the streets, we pay homage to all those who have gone before us, because they truly make us what we are.

Sometimes the children in the area will come over specifically to ask me what decorations I'm putting up. They like my haunted house. They also let me know which fruits and candies they prefer. It seems that apples are preferred over raisins on this block. "Trick or treat!" The little monsters come dressed to kill. They come as Dracula, Frankenstein, and the Wolfman. They come as fairies, as Batman, as Teenage Mutant Ninja Turtles. One very astute young man came to my door wearing a mask of Richard Nixon. Aha! A real monster approaches. We give them apples and candy and sometimes squash.

During the last of the Day of the Dead celebrations, our Women's Society closes the festivities with a celebration of Oya.

Here's how it happened one year: From the outside the house appeared unoccupied. You could barely tell that anything was going on. There were bamboo and raffia shades pulled down at the window, and the candlelight was soft, almost imperceptible. You could feel the mystery. I must have knocked on the door for a solid five minutes before the music was lowered and the dog's barks could be heard. A painted face peeped through the window shade and declared, "Yeye is here." There was the wonderful thunder of women laughing, announcing my arrival, asking why I was late. *Laissez les bontemps rouler*—C'mon, baby, let the good times roll.

I immediately removed my shoes, as is the custom in the homes of our Women's Society members. Then I went over to the chair and slipped out of my blouse and headdress. Bare breasted and bareheaded, half-naked and safe. This was the proper attire for this gathering. Our celebration of the Wildwoman, our party for Oya. I sat for a moment, then went to the kitchen for food. Beans and rice, potato chips, and fruit punch. This was acceptable fun food. For tonight we are without protocol, without taboo. Tonight we will not pray or work or try to figure out the problems of the world. No, not tonight! Tonight we will paint and perfume our bodies. We will dance bare breasted, waving our arms in the wind, screaming for no reason and laughing out loud. Tonight Oya walks through the bush; tonight She dances in the Wind.

I looked at the beautiful bouquet of women assembled in the room. We were short and tall, thick and thin. Some of us were as black as night, some caramel, others were as pale as the moonlight.

Our heads uncovered, our horns exposed! Hair swirled around the room, black and brown, blonde and red, kinky, curly, straight, dread. Long braids flying loose, ornaments wrapped in funny shapes on our heads. All the women of the marketplace were there: We were healers and soldiers, designers and engineers, writers and nurses, teachers and friends, mothers and partners. But tonight we did not work or shop. There was no cleaning or instructing to be done. We only shook our breasts to the rhythm in the wind. Some of these breasts were long and angular, others round and young, some withered and old and even missing due to surgery. Tonight we did not indulge in any ideas of what a "perfect woman" was or should be. Tonight we did not think of our professions, our children, or the problems of the world. For this was the celebration for Oya, and our only concern was to be free like the wild women in the woods.

At Home with the Ancestors

Mother Africa is a vast continent. She holds within Her a natural variety that is almost incomprehensible: scorching desert, open savanna, dense forest, and great mountain ranges. She is the Mother of the Great Beasts, the ancient elephant, the impervious leopard, the graceful gazelle, and the magnificent ape. Here we find the totems of the deities, Isis' mighty vulture, Athena's beloved owl, and Oshun's beautiful parrot. The rivers contain crocodile, fish, and frogs. The water, forest, and sky are populated with critters that fly, buzz, sting, slide, and burrow. Innumerable varieties of plants display sizes and shapes that are among the most amazing to be found in Nature.

Like Africa's land, climate, and wildlife, her people are beautiful and diverse. Some of her children have blue-black skin and dark eyes; others are bronze, umber, or sienna with brown eyes; and in the northern regions they are tan, olive, and vanilla with gray, green, or even blue eyes. They are tall like the Watusi, short like the Pygmy, lean and angular in Nilotic regions, or full-bodied and round-faced in the Congo. They have created many cultures, wear many colors, and speak many languages. But they are all Her children. Undeniably. They have created a great body of myth and folklore and innumerable rituals to express their beliefs about Life and the Afterlife.

Now we'll look at the beliefs about ancestors held by the inhabitants of Venezuela and the Egyptians of the Nile Valley and a few of the people of West Africa. It is not possible to understand or even know all the beliefs of all the people (believe me, I've tried). But this material can help us to understand the relationship between the ancestors and ourselves.

Honoring the Goddess Maria Lionza

A stature of the Goddess Maria Lionza adorns the freeway of Caracas. She is depicted as a beautiful woman riding a great beast (a tapir) and holding a pelvic bone above Her head.

If you don't watch closely you could miss Her standing there like a guardian over the speeding cars as they whiz by. There are roadside shrines dedicated to Her along the Avila Mountain range. But Her most famous shrine is encased in grotto at the top of Mt. Sorte in Yaracuy. That's where I'm going today.

The Lopez family wakes me early and informs me that the journey is long. It takes four hours to drive from the city to the land where Maria Lionza really lives. For miles we drive down the highways, we stop for *arepas* and fruit juice. We play with the ducks and the parrots then get back in the car and wiggle our butts to the music on the radio. Over and over Santana sings, "I'll never go back to Georgia. I'll never go back..." and I wonder, What happened to him in Georgia? Santito explains to me that Latin people sing about everything. I know Black Americans do, too.

Now the highway narrows into a two-lane street, the *casitas* and roadside cafés fade away as sugarcane plantations appear. Then we are heading up into the mountains and the roadside shrines are numerous. Many gifts from many people are nestled between the flowers and the flickering candles lying at the feet of the Queen of the Wilds. The majority of the city's 4 million people are Catholic, but about 50,000 of them journey to the forest to pay homage to Maria during Her annual feast (October 9–13) and throughout the year. Several people I met recounted the myth of the Mother of the Beasts. Here's the short version:

> According to Her devotees, Maria Lionza was the daughter of a Caquetio Indian chief from the region of Nirgua. She was a

167

Autumn

beautiful baby with light-colored eyes, a physical trait that marked her as a bad omen. Tradition required that She be killed at birth, but her father was unable to carry out the sacrifice, so he hid her away in a hut near the lagoon.

As a young woman she went to the lagoon one Sunday and saw her own reflection in the water. She was pleased with Her beauty. But so was the Great Anaconda Snake. He fell in love with Her, kidnapped Her, and pulled Her into the lagoon. There She entered into a mystical marriage with the Snake.

When Her father learned of this union, he attempted to separate Maria from Her serpent-lover. The snake grew and grew till it exploded and became a lake whose waters flooded the land and devastated the people. Then Maria became Protectress of the lake, its environs, and creatures.

Other stories identify her as a White woman. One version says she was the daughter of a Spanish couple who fell in the lake and nearly drowned. *La Onza,* the sacred wildcat (Jaguar) of ancient times, saved her. He impregnated Her with magical powers, and She became Maria La Onza. Another version depicts Her as Maria Alonsa, a stingy landowner of colonial times. It's said She used to hide gold ounces in the mountainside at Sorte. Evidently, she had a change of heart after death and began to grant favors to the people who visited the mountainside. As I listen to the various stories, I think to myself that the second story smells of colonialism and the third sounds like the people's response to it. In my opinion the first story is the best of the three. Meanwhile, much like Oshun and the other Orishas, Maria has taken on the identity of *La Virgen de Coromoto.*

The journey continues until we arrive at the sacred grove. The decorations and the rituals performed here make it clear to me that Maria incorporated Christianity and West African magic into the indigenous belief in Nature spirits. I spent the day with my family climbing the sacred mountain, bathing in the river, and singing in the woods. On the way back to the city we stopped at a roadside stand and bought some fruit that I'd never seen before.

Egyptian Sunset on the Autumn Equinox

Cairo, Egypt, Autumn Equinox, 1999. My question had been answered even before I put foot on Egyptian soil. The answering began in the airport in New York.

I was standing in line at the Egypt Air ticket counter with Jeffrey Mishlove and Kevin Ryerson of the Intuition Network. We were checking luggage and looking over the crowd for the other members of our travel party. Although I sometimes take off for parts unknown alone, going with a group of people on a sacred site tour is my favorite way to travel. I love the interaction that comes with leading rituals on the sites, meeting the people and the spirits, and bringing them together. In this particular moment of waiting in line, though, I was quiet, saying inside my head, I'm going to Egypt! Egypt, whose garden is made of stone. Egypt, whose deities have lived with me for three decades. Egypt, where

Horus was born. Egypt, the land of mystery and magic. This time I'm going to Egypt, where Isis resurrected Osiris. Egypt. *Egypt!!*

Softly a voice whispered behind me. "So, sister, you are going back home." I turned around to see a young Black man, dressed in black pants and a red shirt with a small white cap on his head. He looked directly into my eyes. He was not smiling, but his eyes were twinkling and penetrating mine. I responded with, "Yes, I'm going to Cairo." "I know," he says. "We were there together before . . . remember?"

I had never been to Egypt before, yet a memory began to rumble inside me, an old dream being recalled. I felt that this stranger was someone out of that dream, a stranger who knew the details of it. "Yes, I remember what happened last time," I said, only half-knowing what I was saying. Then he said, "Don't worry. Egypt is in Africa. You're going back home." And then he walked away. Quickly he disappeared in the crowd, reappeared in the distance, then disappeared again. I realized this was no madman, no young man just being fresh. No, this was Elegba, the Messenger who'd come to open the way.

We landed in Cairo, cleared customs, and met our guides, three wonderful gentlemen. They greeted us with "Welcome Home." Every moment of the bus ride to the hotel was extraordinary. Every building seemed mysterious, every statue a spirit looming large against the sky. Every person on the street was a page from *National Geographic* magazine.

Everyone I encountered welcomed me back to Egypt.

Someone asked if my brother would come soon. A little girl on the street scolded me for not wearing my veil. They all thought I was Nubian, and most spoke to me in their own language first, expecting me to understand, and then they changed to English.

Right away the dreams started, the *déjà vu* parade began. I had set up an altar in my hotel room and would say prayers in the morning and salute the altar before I went to bed at night. Every night I would dream the events of the next day. My dreams allowed me to see in advance places I'd never seen before. My dreams told me where to go and what to do, which ritual to perform at each site: a sunrise ritual at the foot of the Sphinx, a story for Obatala at the Pyramids, a song for the ancestors outside the tombs, a dance for Oshun on a boat down the Nile. I saw it all each night before it happened. It was all so clear.

Then Elegba, the Trickster, appeared again.

A ride at Sunset on the Giza plateau was scheduled for the evening of the Autumn Equinox. We piled into the bus and arrived at the stables where horses and camels waited by the side of the road. The guides announced that we had a choice between these two animals. For me the choice was simple and clear. A few nights before I'd had an upsetting dream in which I'd been thrown from a horse. So naturally when this evening arrived I heeded the warning and chose a camel. I was led to a white, long-necked creature named, of all things, Moses, who appeared to look at me with disdain. Mounting a camel is a balancing act. One has to lean forward and back as the camel comes to its feet. I grabbed onto the saddle and raised my right leg, and then my body froze with that leg in mid-air. I flashed back on the dream that had guided my choice. Now I could see that the horse in that dream had a camel's face. I must have bugged my eyes or wrinkled my brow, or I could have actually screamed. Some emotion showed in my face, because the old man in charge of the stable looked at me and said, "Don't be chicken." He signaled for me to mount the camel, and then he handed me the straps.

Now let me tell you something, people. I do all right with fish, birds, cats, dogs, and, occasionally, even a friendly snake. But I am no one's "beast-master." I looked at the strap, then looked at the old man. And the man looked back at me. With a wave of his hand he dismissed my protest and said, "Here, soon you'll remember." With that gesture he connected the strap of the next camel to Moses' saddle, and before I knew it I was leading a caravan across the Giza plateau.

Oh, Elegba, what have you done?

All my life I've been partial to sunsets. In the city, sunsets have kept me sane. But a sunset on the Autumn Equinox in Egypt was more than I could stand. We arrived and dismounted our animals. I looked out into the horizon. The three pyramids stood in the shade. The wind started blowing as the sand shifted beneath my feet. Now I could feel myself flying as if I had great vulture wings. I flew in the sky, I flew into the sand, I even flew under the Earth. Wind and sand and sun and shade, I felt them all at once. And time appeared to stand perfectly still, moved backward and forward, then beyond. I was out of my body and out of my head . . . and out of my mind in my heart.

Someone touched my shoulder, making me return to this time, these people, this place.

Now I had to return to Moses, to mount him, and be on my way. But the disdainful Moses had other ideas. As I clutched on the saddle and mounted his hump, Moses decided to dance. He swung around and intertwined his neck with two other camels, and they began to kiss and do the Camel Walk. I pulled on the rein and Moses ignored me; in fact, I could swear he laughed. I called for the camel drivers to come and untangle us, and with a little effort they did. But Moses looked up and saw the horses in the lead, and he was not to be outdone. So he took off in a gallop, pulling the caravan into the setting sun. Oh, Elegba.

I had longed to go to Egypt for thirty years, and now that I was there, I knew that I was home.

The Ancestors of the future

Both the Egyptians and the Yorubas of West Africa believed that when a person died the individual would dissolve, but fragments of the Eternal spirit within would continue. When a person died, their heart was measured against the weight of a white Ostrich feather on the scales of a Goddess named Maat. If the scales balanced, the soul could be elevated to a higher state of being. (I guess it pays to stay light-hearted.) If deification was in order, it included an elaborate burial at which great sacrifices were made, elaborate offerings given, and elegant processions done. Deification preserved the godlike substance of the dead person.

The Egyptians and the Yorubas believed that animals and plants also had souls. Each Pharaoh was seen as a personification of the falcon-headed deity Horus, the Son born of Isis's and Osiris's miraculous conception.

The deification process is practiced in many places. Usually, it is done after death (immediately or years later), but on rare occasions a person may be deified during his or her lifetime. Chaka, the Zulu warrior who united South Africa, was deified in his own lifetime. In Haiti the Voudou *loa* known as Dan Petro was an eighteenth-century *houngan* (priest). The Catholic Church deifies (canonizes) its saints, as do the Buddhists. With the help of modern media we make demigods of political figures and movie stars, and even romanticize famous criminals.

In Yorubaland, the Egungun society attends to the business of proper burial for royalty, priests, and ordinary people according to their position and their accomplishments in this life. During the Ancestral Season, the society sponsors elaborate masquerades to honor the memory of the ancestors. They dress in elegant regalia, and they reenact the mythic dramas from the ancestors' lives. These village theater performances continue throughout the day and night. Some are solemn, some joyous. Some go on for three to thirty-one days nonstop. Now there's a costume ball. A modern version of this masquerade is performed by the students of my

"Art of Ancestral Drama" class on November 1. This is the show that Katarina, mentioned earlier, attends.

The African bush is regarded not only as a physical place in Nature (the forest) but also as a mystical place. The real forest is populated with plants, animals, and mythic beings; the mystical forest houses the beliefs, fears, and dreams of the human psyche.

Both forces and ideas become personified through human thought and action. If the thought and action associated with an individual have a profound effect on the collective, that person becomes a legendary figure, like Jesus Christ. So today many people regard Mahatma Gandhi, John F. Kennedy, Harriet Tubman, Martin Luther King, Jr., Sojourner Truth, John Coltrane, Joan of Arc, and El Hadj Malik El Shabazz Malcolm X (just to name a few) as symbols of Freedom. This is one road to deification. On the other hand, the swastika, an ancient sacred symbol, now signifies the degenerative cruelty of Hitler. He walked the path not of deification but of demonization. On a daily basis "little people" like you and me perform heroic deeds. We must realize that we are the "ancestors of the future."

If we perform our job well enough, our collective effort will be mythologized in the folklore of the future. Sow well, that we may reap a bountiful harvest. Go deep into the roots of your past, live well, and celebrate life, so that your Jump Up will reach the stars in the sky.

Suggestions for Celebrating Autumn

The Autumn Crown

Here's a simple project for the kids: Take an old hat and decorate it using construction paper and cardboard. Cut out a Sundisk and cowhorns to make an Isis crown. Use autumn leaves, cinnamon sticks, and pumpkin seeds to make an Oya crown. These can be glued, sown, stapled, and tucked with just a little help from parents.

The Seasonal Table

Autumn is one of the most pleasurable seasons for decorating. An abundance of seasonal fabrics and tablecloths depicting the harvest are available at your local stores. Wreaths of dried spices and cornucopias abound as well as ornamental corn and gourds. Choose any of these and assemble them for your holiday table.

The Seasonal Altar

For an altar, you may want to add a special centerpiece for the Roman Goddess Ceres, the Queen of Grains, from whom our breakfast cereal gets its name.

Get a large platter (preferably a large round one) and line it with leaves or straw. Put a pumpkin or eggplant in the center of the platter. Then place ¼ cup of grain and the colored candle in the directions as follows:

Rice in the East, with a yellow candle

Millet in the South, with a red candle

Corn in the West, with an orange candle

Wheat in the North, with a brown candle.

Address the spirit of the grain in each direction and light the candle:

> We call to this gathering the spirit of Rice, of the ancestors who watered the fields. Come and be with us.
>
> We call to this gathering the spirit of Millet, of the ancestors who separated the seeds.
>
> We call to this gathering the spirit of Corn, of the ancestors who harvested the ears.
>
> We call to this gathering the spirit of Wheat, the ancestors who ground it into flour.
>
> We, at this gathering, give thanks to the Earth, to the ancestors, and to the Sun.
>
> We give thanks for our strength, our abundance, and our joy. Blessing to all.

An Autumn Ritual

This ritual I call "Sweeping the Cemetery."

It is an old New Orleans custom to wash, paint (white), and decorate the vaults (built above ground) in the cemetery. Sometimes family members will light candles, bring food, and have a picnic with loved ones in the cemetery. One of the most important rituals my family performs is that of sweeping the cemetery and attending neglected graves. If your family wishes, you may perform a similar ritual.

Preparation

For this ritual you will need the following things. Take all of them to the cemetery with you.

A broom

Nine pennies

A large bouquet of flowers

A white candle (in a glass)

A garbage bag

A jar of saltwater

A hand towel

Performing the Ritual

The Broom: Before you leave your house, take a regular household broom (preferably a new one) and decorate it with nine strips of ribbon of different colors. Fasten the ribbons to the whisk part of the broom. Sprinkle or spray the broom with rum or other spirits. This broom goes to the cemetery with you.

Entering the Cemetery: As you approach the gateway of the cemetery, knock three times, asking the gatekeeper for permission to enter. You may address the gatekeeper as Elegba, Ghede-Nibo, St. Peter, or simply "the gatekeeper." When you feel you have permission, turn around in a circle, scraping your feet against the ground as if cleaning your shoes. Then face the gate and throw three pennies over the threshold of the gate. Step in.

Finding Your Territory: Most cemeteries have a paupers' or John Doe section where poor people or those who were buried free are deposited, and you might want to do this ritual there. Or you may simply look for a neglected area. Establish a starting place by placing the white candle on the ground at that spot. Light the candle and speak to the spirits in that area. State your name and your intention, making it clear that you are not a thief and that you have come to "settle the stirring."

Sweeping the Cemetery: Now use your broom to sweep the graveyard. Pick up dead flowers, bottles, cans, and other debris and place them in the garbage bag. Sweep smaller particles away from the gravestones. Clear paths and tidy up walkways. Avoid sweeping anyone's feet, including your own.

Placing the Flowers: Now lay a few flowers on as many graves as you've cleaned in that area. If the headstones have names, pronounce the names of the ancestors. As you lay the flower down, say, "Mojuba. Love and respect to you, Ms. Mary Jones." If you have the urge to talk, do so. If you have the urge to listen, do so. Shake out the broom. Throw the garbage bag in a receptacle inside the cemetery, or the nearest receptacle outside the cemetery. Snuff the candle out with wet fingers. (You will later burn the candle at home on your ancestor shrine.) Gather up yourself and your things. As you leave this area, throw three pennies behind you.

Leaving the Cemetery: As you approach the gate (please leave by the same gate you entered), stop on the graveyard side of the threshold. Open the jar of salt water. Wet your hands and sprinkle the water around yourself. Clean your aura by sprinkling water over your entire body, starting at the top of your head, and spilling some on your shoes. Dry your hands. Face the cemetery and ask the spirits to let there be peace and tranquility in the neighborhood. Step over the threshold. Throw the last three pennies over your left shoulder. Walk away and don't look back.

An Autumn Recipe: Quick and Easy Mooncakes

Akara is offered to the ancestors in Nigeria, Brazil, and the United States. Akara is a deep-fried fritter similar to hushpuppies and hot-water cornbread. Handmade akara is a time-consuming process, and some elders insist that things be done "the old-fashioned way."

Directions the Old-Fashioned Way

It begins by selecting the finest black-eyed peas. They are washed as songs are sung. Then they are soaked overnight (preferably in spring water). The next day the skins are removed and the pounding, an act usually performed by women, begins. The beans are placed in a large mortar and pestle and pounded into a mush. In Africa, during this process women sing bare breasted. In Brazil the beans are boiled then mashed into mush. The mush is seasoned and deep-fat fried, then arranged on a plate and served to the ancestors.

Directions the Quick and Easy Way

I used to make akara the "old-fashioned way," but over the years

I've convinced my ancestors to accept the quick and easy way:

Purchase a tub of organic firm tofu. Chill it a day or two in advance to assure firmness. Drain the water off, then cut the bean-cake into ¼ inch slices (or thicker if you please). Season the slices and fry.

Spice Options

Spicing akara is a symbolic language in itself. For example:

Spice it with hot things such as pepper sauce or fresh ginger, and dust it with cornmeal if you're asking the ancestors for strength or protection.

Flavor the tofu with vanilla and roll it in sesame seeds if you are asking for blessing or giving thanks for those already received.

Add a little honey and cinnamon if you're asking for love.

Serve the akara on a bed of green leaves and garnish with coins if you're praying for abundance.

At one time my ancestors insisted upon being served acorn bread. It was quite a job finding acorn flour. Think about your ancestors and meditate on the issues at hand, then make the akara. You may want to serve it at the Dumb Supper.

The Dumb Supper

Cook a meal consisting of food from your ancestral culture. Usually this kind of cooking is done in total silence, but you can sing if you make the akara (described before) bare breasted.

Set the table with a place setting for each human participating.

181

Autumn

Put a special place setting in the center of the table. This plate contains dirt from the cemetery with a white candle in its center. Participants may invoke the directions and bless the food at 11:55 P.M. Place a little of each dish on the central plate, then leave the room and do not return until 12:05 A.M. This gives the spirits the opportunity to eat first. When the humans return to the table, they may eat in silence. At meal's end, the contents of the central plate may be placed on the ancestor shrine, left in the cemetery, or put in the compost.

for Every Season

Every season brings with it a particular blessing:

> The quiet of winter
>
> The colors of autumn
>
> The freedom of summer
>
> The joy of spring.

And though I have learned to respond to each gift:

> By exploring the depths of my dreams in winter
>
> By harvesting the abundance of my work in autumn
>
> By connecting to kindred and running free in summer
>
> I confess that I love spring best of all.

> Now it is April 2000, dear reader, and I am standing beneath
> a cherry tree in Tokyo. You are here with me as you have been
> all along. We walked together on the beach in Borneo, drinking
> in the blue of the sky and the ocean. We wrapped ourselves in
> silk batiks in Malaysia and kissed heart-shaped leaves in the rain
> forest.

If you hold my hand, be still, and listen we can hear fresh water running down the falls into the river that leads to the sea; drums beating in the bush; barefoot women dancing in the villages; and birds singing in our own back yards.

Let us take a deep breath, plant our feet firmly in the Earth, lift our faces to the Heavens, and feel the full embrace of Our Blessing. Here beneath the cherry tree the winds of change blow as pink and white blossoms shower down upon us. Let us drink deeply of this beauty and abundance of spring. Let us give thanks for the coming of another year and the opportunity to jump up again.

CALENDAR of CELEBRATIONS

January

1 New Year's Day / Celebration of Bembe Elegba / Kwanzaa ends	**2**	**3**	**4**	**5** Kore's Day
6 Epiphany / Thor's Day	**7** Sekhmet's Day	**8** Druid New Year	**9** Festival of Janus	**10**
11 Banba War Goddess	**12**	**13**	**14** Tamil Thai Pongal	**15** Feast of the Ass
16 Martin Luther King, Jr. Day	**17** St. Anthony's Day	**18** Surya Hindu Sun Deities	**19** Thorrablottar— Husband's Day	**20** Festival of the Kitchen God
21 St. Agnes' Day	**22** St. Vincent and the Grenadine's Day	**23** Festa do Bonfim	**24**	**25**
26 Festival of Ekedo	**27**	**28** Up-Helly-Aa Scottish Fire Festival	**29** Hikuli Dance Festival of Peace	**30**
31 Hecate's Feast				

February

1 St. Brigit's Day	**2** Candlemas	**3** Powamu Festival	**4**	**5** St. Agatha's Day
6 Feast of Aphrodite	**7**	**8** Dakini Day	**9** Spring Festival Argungu Fishing Festival	**10** Our Lady of Lourdes
11 Festival of Artemis	**12**	**13** St. Valentine's Day	**14** Lupercalia	**15** Festival of Sarasvati
16 Festival of Fornax, the Goddess of Bread and Ovens	**17** Keeper of the Earth Festival	**18** Kiddies Carnival	**19**	**20** Tincunaco Ceremony
21 St. Lucia's Day	**22**	**23** Feast of Kali	**24** Time of the Old Woman	**25**
26	**27** Feast of Esther / Day of Selene	**28**	**29**	

March

		1	2	3	4	5
		Matronalia begins	Japanese Doll Festival Japanese Peach Festival	Mothering Day	Kite Festival Celebration of Isis	
6 Matronalia ends Four Miracles Day	**7** Junoalia	**8** International Women's Day	**9** Celebration of Aphrodite and Adonis	**10** Festival of Holi	**11** Hara Ke Johnny Appleseed Day	**12** St. Gregory's Day
13 Purification Feast	**14** Fallas de San Jose	**15**	**16** Purim Dionysus Festival	**17** St. Patrick's Day	**18** Ibu Afo Festival	**19** Aganyu St. Joe the Worker's Day Feast of Minerva Athena's Day
20 Feast of Ostara	**21** Spring Equinox Mothering Day	**22**	**23** Summer Finding Festival of Isis	**24**	**25** Hilaria's Day	**26** Plowing Day
27 Feast of Kuan Yin	**28**	**29** Ishtar Festival Bobo Masquerade	**30**	**31** Feast of Luna (Roman Moon Goddess)		

April

		1	2	3	4	5
		April Fools' Day Feast of Fortuna	Children's Book Day	Buddha's Birthday		Tomb-Sweeping Day Festival of Fortuna
6 Boat Festival	**7** World Health Day	**8**	**9** A-Ma Fisherman	**10**	**11** Feast of San Leo	**12** Cerealia begins
13 Sinhala Tamil New Year/ Songkran	**14** Maryamma (Hindu Sea Goddess)	**15** Festival of Ba'ast	**16** Asase Yaa	**17** Chariot Festival	**18** Rava Navami	**19** Cerealia ends
20 Yaqui Pagean	**21**	**22** Earth Day	**23** St. George's Day	**24** Children's Day	**25**	**26**
27 Tyi Wara Feast of the Farmers	**28** Floralia begins	**29** Floralia Sham-al-Neseem	**30** Floralia May Eve Beltane begins at sundown			

May

1 Floralia ends / Feast of St. Joseph / Our Lady of Peace and Good Voyages begins	**2**	**3** Corn Festival	**4** St. Monica's Day	**5** Feast of the Banners
6	**7**	**8**	**9** Lemuria	**10** Bun Bang Fai Broom Day
11	**12** Indian Forest God Sashti	**13** Our Lady of Fatima	**14** Isis Day	**15** Rain Dance Night
16	**17** Nejma Health and Healing Day Santa Clara	**18**	**19** Yoruba Ibeji Ceremony	**20**
21 Day of Tefnut	**22**	**23**	**24** Po Ino Nogar Furrow Day	**25**
26 Cordelia	**27** Festival of Sulis at Bath	**28**	**29**	**30** Memorial Day Joan of Arc
31 Our Lady of Peace and Good Voyages ends				

June

1 International Children's Day	**2** Gawai Dayak	**3** Broken Dolls Day Bellona	**4** Juvenalia	**5** Sheela-Na-Gig
6 Moslem Night of Observation	**7** Rice Festival	**8**	**9** Field Day	**10** Day of Anahita
11 Mater Matuta	**12** Festival of Mut	**13**	**14** Birthday of the Muses	**15** Day of St. Vitus
16 Tano Children's Festival	**17** Couple's Day Japanese Lily Festival	**18**	**19**	**20** Feast of Ix Chel
21 Juneteenth Summer Solstice Yemaya's Day	**22**	**23** St. John's Eve	**24** Feast of the Sun Feast of St. John the Baptist	**25** Tartar Festival of the Plow
26 Alaskan Whale Dance	**27** Day of the Seven Sleepers	**28** St. Peter and St. Paul's Day	**29**	**30**

July

		1	2	3	4	5
		Canada Day	Visitation of Our Lady	Seminole Green Corn Dance	Independence Day	Sun Dance Festival
6	**7**	**8**	**9**	**10**	**11**	**12**
	Feast of Juno	St. Elizabeth's Day		Pilgrimage of Saut d'eau	Feast of Min	Yatra
13	**14**	**15**	**16**	**17**	**18**	**19**
Obon Festival begins Reed Dance Day	Bastille Day	Obon Festival ends	Our Lady of Carmel	Amaterasu (Sun Goddess) Birthday of Isis	Birthday of Nephthys	Egyptian New Year
20	**21**	**22**	**23**	**24**	**25**	**26**
Binding of the Wreaths	Mayan New Year	Choctaw Festival	Egyptian Dog Days	Simon Bolivar's Birthday		Hopi Kachina Dance Feast of St Anne
27	**28**	**29**	**30**	**31**		
Peruvian Independence Day	St. Martha's Day		Lammas Eve			

August

		1	2	3	4	5
		Honowo Hooting at Hunger	Feast of the Black Madonna	Drimes	Feast of the Blessed Virgin Mary	
6	**7**	**8**	**9**	**10**	**11**	**12**
Festival of Thoth	Breaking of the Nile	Naga Panchami	Seven Sister Festival	Double Seven Day	Shooting Star Night	Light of Isis
13	**14**	**15**	**16**	**17**	**18**	**19**
Hecate's Day		Feast of the Assumption	Ramadan	Festival of Diana	St. Helen's Day	Vinalia/Festival of Jupiter
20	**21**	**22**	**23**	**24**	**25**	**26**
Hopi Flute Ceremony		Day of Moira (Goddess of Fate) Festival of Vulcan and the Nymphs			Feast of Ops	
27	**28**	**29**	**30**	**31**		
Procession of Bast Krishna	Harvest Festival	Gelede Festival Feast of Ogun	Saint Rose of Lima	Eyo Masquerade		

September

		1 Feast of the First Fruit	2 Odwira	3 Akwambo Path Clearing	4 Sunrise Dance	5 Ganesh Chaturti
6 Our Lady of the Remedies	7 Feast of Durga Feast of Yemaya and Oshun	8 International Literacy Day	9 Flower Festival Horn Dance	10	11 Cure Salee Day of Queens	12 Coptic New Year 2
13	14 Feast of the Black Madonna Fire Lighting Ceremony Feast of Lights	15 Onam Chang O Yam Festival begins Acorn Festival	16 Mid-Autumn Festival	17 Monkey Festival	18	19 Yam Festival
20 Kite Flying	21	22 Ho Khao Slak Autumn Equinox	23	24 Annual Death and Rebirth of Osiris	25	26
27 Sts. Cosmas and Damian	28	29 St. Michael's Day	30 Ibo Issa Aka Hand Washing Ritual			

October

		1 Gandhi's Birthday	2 Tangun	3 Elk Festival Jejunium Cereris	4 Nairobi Show	5
6 Zapopan Mexican Rain Goddess	7 Fantasia	8 Gai Jatra Cow Festival	9 Felicitas' Day (Roman Goddess of Joy) Feast of Maria Lionza begins	10 Ra'l Ra'l Festival of Lights begins	11 Vinalia Wine Festival	12 Fortuna Redux
13 Floating of the Lamps Feast of Maria Lionza ends	14	15 Sacred Harvest Festival	16 World Food Day	17 Festival of the Grains	18 Horned God Ancestral Season begins	19
20 Chinese Ancestor Festival	21 Misisi Beer Festival	22 Rain Making Ceremony	23 Swallows of San Juan Capistrano Day	24 United Nations Day	25 St. Crispin's Day	26 Felicitastas
27 Feast of Holy Souls	28 Potato Day Ceremonies for Isis begin	29	30 Mayan Angels Day	31 Halloween		

November

			1 All Saints' Day Day of the Dead	2 All Souls' Day Ancestral Season ends	3 Gaelic New Year	4 Mischief Night	5
6 Feast of Tiamat St. Leonard's Day	7 Makahiki Harvest Festival	8 Festival of the Kitchen Goddess	9 Thai Feast of Lights	10 Goddess of Reason	11 Queen of the Fairies	12	
13 Jupiter Festival	14	15	16	17 Feast of St. Hilda	18	19 Santa Isabel	
20 United Nations Child's Day	21 Old Veiled Woman	22 Feast of St. Cecilia	23 Togo Habye Festival	24 Feast of the Burning Lamps	25 Feast of St. Catherine	26 Tibetan Festival of Lights Basari Manhood Rite	
27	28 Day of Sophia Goddess of Wisdom	29	30 Day of Mawu				

December

			1 Festival of Poseidon	2 Pan American Health Day	3 Feast of Fauna	4 Feast of Shango	5 Sinterklaas Day St. Nicholas Eve
6 St. Nicholas' Day	7 Mummers' Plays	8 Feast of the Immaculate Conception	9 Festival of Tonantzin	10 Goddess of Liberty Festival	11 Day of Coatlique	12 Feast Day for the Virgin of Guadalupe	
13 Luciadagen	14 Hopi Blue Corn Dance	15 Consus	16 Las Posadas begins	17 Saturnalia begins	18 Misa de Aquinaldo	19 Sarasvati	
20 Mother's Night	21 Mayan New Year	22 Incwala Kingship Ceremony Festival of Lights	23 Night of the Radishes	24 Christmas Eve Las Posades ends Saturnalia ends	25 Christmas Day Celebration of Astarte Jevenalia (Children's Day)	26 Kwanzaa begins	
27	28	29	30 Imanje New Year's Eve	31			

ACKNOWLEDGMENTS

My sincerest thanks go to:

The entire staff of Conari Press, especially Mary Jane Ryan, Will Glennon, Leslie Berriman, and Brenda Knight.

Ms. Shirley Lee, who taught me how to overcome and succeed.

Jeffrey Mishlove, Kevin Ryerson, Emile, Medhut, and Muhammad, who took me home to Egypt.

Dr. William Ruch and Dr. Mina Karimabadi, who kept me healthy while I worked.

Iya Oshunyade and Iya Efunyemi, who helped me preserve my last nerve.

Caroline Durston, Sylvia Warren, and the spirits of the River.

Baba Fatalami, the warrior poet.

Maurillio Gonzalez, the mad *congero*.

Iyanla Vanzant, for stories shared.

My husband, Awo Falokun Fatunmbi, for patience and endurance.

The Spirit Women's Actualization Group, for years and years of sisterhood and support. I couldn't have done it without you.

NOTES

1. Pauline Campanelli. *Wheel of the Year: Living the Magical Life* (St. Paul, MN: Llewellyn Publications, 1989), p. 6.

2. Marion Green. *A Calendar of Festivals: Traditional Celebrations, Songs, Seasonal Recipes, and Things to Make* (Rockport, MA: Element Inc., 1991), p. 133.

3. Lyle Saxon, Robert Tallant, and Edward Dreyer. *Gumbo Ya Ya: A Collection of Louisiana Folktales* (New York: Bonanza, 1945), p. 19.

4. Saxon, et al. *Gumbo Ya Ya,* p. 3.

5. Herbert Thurston and Donald Attwater, eds. *Butler's Lives of the Saints* (New York: Kennedy, 1956), p. 632.

6. Murry Hope. *Practical Egyptian Magic* (New York: St. Martin's Press, 1984), pp. 69-70.

7. Personal interview with Santos and Chefe Lopez, at La Casa de la Poesia, Caracas, Venezuela, July 1999.

Bibliography

Badejo, Diedre. *Osun Seegesi: The Elegant Deity of Wealth, Power, and Femininity.* Trenton NJ: Africa World Press, 1996.

Bibbs, Susheel. *Heritage of Power.* San Francisco: MEP Publications, 1998.

Budapest, Zsuzsanna E. *The Grandmother of Time.* San Francisco: HarperSanFrancisco, 1989.

Campanelli, Pauline. *Wheel of the Year: Living the Magical Life.* St. Paul, MN: Llewellyn Publications, 1989.

Coleman, Will. *Tribal Talk.* University Park, PA: Pennsylvania State University Press, 2000.

Conway, D. J. *Moon Magick: Myth and Magic, Crafts and Recipes, Rituals and Spells.* St. Paul, MN: Llewellyn Publications, 1997.

Cooper, J. C. *The Aquarian Dictionary of Festivals.* Wellingborough, England: The Aquarian Press, 1990.

Cunningham, Scott. *The Magic in Food: Legend, Lore, and Spellwork.* St. Paul, MN: Llewellyn Publications, 1991.

Edwards, Carolyn McVickar. *Sun Stories: Tales from Around the World to Illuminate the Days and Nights of Our Lives.* San Francisco: HarperSanFrancisco, 1995.

Fatunmbi, Awo Falokun. *Iba'se Orisa: Ifa Proverbs, Folktales, Sacred History, and Prayer.* Original publication, 1994.

Green, Marion. *A Calendar of Festivals: Traditional Celebrations, Songs, Seasonal Recipes, and Things to Make.* Rockport, MA: Element Inc., 1991.

Monaghan, Patricia. *The Book of Goddesses and Heroines.* New York: E. P. Dutton, 1981.

Murry, Hope. *Practical Egyptian Magic.* New York: St. Martin's Press, 1984.

Rufus, Anneli. *The World Holiday Book: Celebrations for Every Day of the Year.* San Francisco: HarperSanFrancisco, 1994.

Saxon, Lyle, with Robert Tallant and Edward Dreyer. *Gumbo Ya Ya: A Collection of Louisiana Folktales.* New York: Bonanza, 1945.

Sjoo, Monica, and Barbara Mor. *The Great Cosmic Mother: Rediscovering the Religion of the Earth.* San Francisco: Harper & Row, 1987.

Stone, Merlin. *Ancient Mirrors of Womanhood: Our Goddess and Heroine Heritage.* Vols. I and II. New York: New Sibylline Books, 1979.

Teish, Luisah. *Carnival of the Spirit: Seasonal Celebrations and Rites of Passage.* San Francisco: HarperSanFrancisco, 1994.

Telesco, Patricia. *365 Goddess: A Daily Guide to the Magic and Inspiration of the Goddess.* San Francisco: HarperSanFrancisco, 1998.

Van Straalen, Alice. *The Book of Holidays Around the World.* New York: E. P. Dutton, 1986.

INDEX

S

St. John the Baptist, 84, 119–29
St. Joseph, 35, 74, 83–5, 121
St. Nicholas, 36–7, 39
San Francisco, xi, 159
Santa Claus, 36–7, 40
Saturnalia, 34, 80
Scorpio, 158
seasons (*see also specific seasons:* Sun) xi–xii
serpents (*see also* Damballah Hwedo) 12, 18, 92, 168
Sesheta, 134
Set, *see* Isis
Shango, 30, 53, 89, 103, 160–1
shekere, 28
Shinto, 115
Sirius, 134, 137
solstices (*see also* summer; winter) xii–xiii
Sophia, 134
South Africa, 174
South America, 18
Spanish, 116, 122
spring, 15–6, 20, 30, 65–104
    equinox, xii, 71–4, 77, 85–7
    Spring Maiden, 15, 72–4, 82, 115
Starhawk, 6, 91, 159
suggestions for celebrating
    autumn, 176–82
    spring, 94–104
    summer, 137–42
    winter, 51–64
summer, 15, 107–42
    solstice, xiii, 72, 114–8, 121, 150
    and St. John's Eve, 121–9
    suggestions for celebrating, 137–42
Sun (*see also* summer) 5, 11–3, 76, 114–8, 128
    and moon, 92–3, 117–8
    and calendar, xii–xiii, 32–3
Surma, 117
Sweden, 115
"sweeping the cemetery" 177–80
Switzerland, 150

T

table
    for autumn, 176
    for spring, 97

Z

ABOUT THE AUTHOR

Luisah Teish is a writer, performer, priestess of Oshun (the West African Goddess of Love, Art, and Sensuality), and ritual designer. She is the author of *Jambalaya: The Natural Women's Book of Personal Charms and Practical Rituals*. She teaches Women's Rites of Passage, Femmyth, and Ritual at the University of Creation Spirituality, Naropa Oakland, John F. Kennedy University, and New College of California. She has performed mythplays and folk storytelling in the United States, Canada, Europe, Australia, and New Zealand.

To Our Readers

Conari Press publishes books on topics ranging from spirituality, personal growth, and relationships to women's issues, parenting, and social issues. Our mission is to publish quality books that will make a difference in people's lives—how we feel about ourselves and how we relate to one another. We value integrity, compassion, and receptivity, both in the books we publish and in the way we do business.

As a member of the community, we sponsor the Random Acts of Kindness™ Foundation, the guiding force behind Random Acts of Kindness™ Week. We donate our damaged books to nonprofit organizations, dedicate a portion of our proceeds from certain books to charitable causes, and continually look for new ways to use natural resources as wisely as possible.

Our readers are our most important resource, and we value your input, suggestions, and ideas about what you would like to see published. Please feel free to contact us, to request our latest book catalog, or to be added to our mailing list.

2550 Ninth Street, Suite 101

Berkeley, California 94710-2551

800-685-9595 510-649-7175

fax: 510-649-7190   e-mail: conari@conari.com

www.conari.com